# Antisemitism in Europe
## Challenging Official Indifference

By Michael McClintock & Judith Sunderland

human rights *first*
THE NEW NAME OF
LAWYERS COMMITTEE FOR HUMAN RIGHTS

## About Us

For the past quarter century, Human Rights First (the new name of Lawyers Committee for Human Rights) has worked in the United States and abroad to create a secure and humane world by advancing justice, human dignity and respect for the rule of law. We support human rights activists who fight for basic freedoms and peaceful change at the local level; protect refugees in flight from persecution and repression; help build a strong international system of justice and accountability; and make sure human rights laws and principles are enforced in the United States and abroad.

## Acknowledgements

This report was written by Michael McClintock and Judith Sunderland. Martina Pomeroy assisted in its research and production. Michael McClintock and Eric Biel edited the report. Cover and book design by Sarah Graham.

We want to acknowledge the invaluable assistance of the many organizations and individuals who offered advice and assisted us in compiling the facts reflected in the report.

We in particular want to thank Michael Whine (Community Security Trust, United Kingdom), Elisabeth Cohen-Tannoudji of the Conseil Représentatif des Institutions juives de France, CRIF, Suzette Bronkhorst and Ronald Eissens (Magenta Foundation Complaints Bureau for Discrimination on the Internet), Deirdre Berger (American Jewish Committee, Berlin Office), Alexey Korotaev (International League for Human Rights), Panayote Dimitras (Greek Helsinki Monitor), Heike Radvan (Amadeu Antonio Stiftung, Germany), and Sirpa Rautio (Office of Democratic Institutions and Human Rights, OSCE). We would like in particular to thank Felice Gaer, Sybil Kessler, and Allison Cohen of the Jacob Blaustein Institute for the Advancement of Human Rights for their contribution to the preparation of this report.

Finally, we wish to thank the Ford Foundation, the John D. and Catherine T. MacArthur Foundation, the John Merck Fund, and the JEHT Foundation, whose financial support made this report possible.

This report is available online at www.HumanRightsFirst.org.
For more information about the report or to purchase it please contact:
Email: Pubs@HumanRightsFirst.org  or Tel.: (212) 845-5275

**New York Headquarters**
Human Rights First
333 Seventh Avenue
13th Floor
New York, NY 10001

Tel: (212) 845-5200
Fax: (212) 845-5299

www.HumanRightsFirst.org

**Washington, DC Office**
Human Rights First
100 Maryland Avenue, N.E.
Suite 502
Washington, DC 20002

Tel: (202) 547-5692
Fax: (202) 543-5999

# Table of Contents

Foreword ...................................................... i

Executive Summary ............................... vii

Introduction ................................................ 1

Antisemitism in Europe:
Challenging Official Indifference ................... 5

A Country by Country Snapshot ................... 27

    Austria ................................................ 29

    Belgium ............................................. 31

    Denmark ........................................... 35

    France ................................................ 37

    Germany ............................................ 41

    Italy ................................................... 45

    Latvia ................................................ 47

    The Netherlands ................................ 51

    Russian Federation ........................... 53

    Sweden .............................................. 59

    United Kingdom ............................... 61

International Standards ............................... 63

A Human Rights First Publication

A "New Antisemitism"? ........................................67

Recommendations ................................................77

Endnotes ................................................................ 81

A Human Rights First Publication

# Foreword

As new reports come from Europe of anti-Jewish bombings, arson, personal assaults, and ongoing incitement to violence, efforts to place antisemitism squarely on the international human rights agenda are beginning to make progress. On April 28 in Berlin, 55 mostly-European governments will meet to discuss these issues, and to explore collective responses. This report is addressed to those governments. It presents a snapshot of the problem of antisemitism in Europe today and proposes a set of practical recommendations to governments. In so doing it seeks to confront a pattern of official indifference which has too often characterized their response to this very serious human rights problem.

The smashed windows and graffiti-daubed walls of burned out Jewish schools, shops, community centers, and synagogues have been among the most striking signs of the violence. These appear against a backdrop of hundreds of attacks on ordinary people that go largely unreported, and a climate of intimidation and fear in which the possibility of attack terrorizes whole communities.

These violent attacks are fueled by an increasingly ugly political climate, where antisemitic rhetoric permeates rallies and other public discourse. Often the spoken or written word incites, accompanies, and celebrates the window-breaking, the fire-bombings, and the beatings – and gives resonance to its racist intent.

This report focuses on the monitoring and reporting of antisemitic violence and threats of violence in Europe – and the corresponding failure of European governments to enforce their laws aimed at stopping these attacks. Our emphasis on monitoring is intended to throw light on a particular failing of European governments in their response to racist violence. This is not to understate the need for education in tolerance, for a responsible news media, and for the criminal justice systems to detect, punish, and prevent hate crimes. Our point is that timely, accurate, and public information on racist violence is an essential first step in developing effective action to suppress it.

The rise of antisemitism in Europe has come to a head in the last three years, as a wave of hate crimes against Jewish people and institutions surged across the region. The attacks extended from the Welsh city of Swansea to the neighborhoods of Paris and the outskirts of Moscow (and on, to the port city of Vladivostok on the Pacific). The level of violence increased significantly in the course of 2002 and continues today at a high level in many parts of Europe.

Two years ago Human Rights First wrote about these issues in a report entitled *Fire and Broken Glass: The Rise of Antisemitism in Europe*. Inexplicably, this extraordinary violence against Jews was both seriously under-reported and largely characterized by governments as a transitory side-effect of the Middle East conflict. Members of the Jewish community in France, for example, were advised by government officials that the best course of action was for them simply to keep a low profile. Antisemitic threats and violence were largely absent from the antiracism agendas of European governments and institutions even as the violence proliferated. There was relatively little reporting in mainstream media beyond coverage of a few high-profile incidents, often linking the violence to hostility between Muslims and Jews.

In *Fire and Broken Glass* we documented and reported upon anti-Jewish violence and government responses through the lens of international human rights standards. We looked in particular at government monitoring and reporting of racist violence as a point of departure to address the failure of governments to fulfill their international legal obligations to fight racism.

In doing so, we aimed also to raise awareness and to press for concrete measures to combat all forms of racist violence in Europe at a time in which anti-immigrant violence, in particular, was on the rise. By emphasizing monitoring and reporting we have identified needed areas of improvement that should benefit all of the minority communities that are victims of racism.

The report also showed that with a few exceptions, national governments, intergovernmental organizations, and nongovernmental organizations had not responded adequately to the growing scourge of antisemitism. A result was an information deficit on hate crimes, with most European governments failing even to provide basic reporting on the crimes that force many in Europe's Jewish communities to live in fear.

The information deficit concealed the real incidence of hate crimes – even though simple observation and the reporting of community organizations made clear that crimes driven by anti-Jewish animus were of extreme severity and increasing in number. Better documentation alone, of course, will accomplish little if governmental authorities do not strengthen their laws barring such crimes, and investigate and prosecute those who are responsible.

Finally, it was our view then, and remains our view today, that the human rights movement needs to come together to confront the rise of antisemitism in Europe. Antisemitism is a violation of human rights. It is part of a much larger global pattern of discrimination which does not receive the attention it deserves. While antisemitic violence and attacks have been well reported by Jewish organizations like the American Jewish Committee, the Anti-Defamation League, and the Union of Councils for Jews of the Former Soviet Union (known as UCSJ), the broader rights community has not addressed these issues with the urgency they deserve.

This, too, is beginning to change. In June, 2003, the Organization for Security and Cooperation in Europe (OSCE) held its first ever special meeting on antisemitism, in Vienna. Human Rights First was a part of the large and diverse group of participants from the human rights movement there, and, with other partner organizations, has been part of a working group convened by the Jacob Blaustein Institute for the Advancement of Human Rights to follow up the conference.

At the Berlin meeting of the OSCE, Human Rights First is proud to be part of a delegation organized by the Leadership Conference on Civil Rights, the oldest, largest, and most diverse civil and human rights coalition in the United States. The Leadership Conference is comprised of over 185 organizations representing the interests of racial and ethnic minorities, women, organized labor, individuals with disabilities, older Americans, major religious groups, gays and lesbians and civil liberties and human rights groups. It is ideally suited to galvanize greater attention to the problem of antisemitism and to link antisemitism to a broader pattern of global discrimination.

The Leadership Conference's delegation at Berlin will include, among others, representatives of the American Association of Persons with Disabilities, Global Rights, the Jewish Council for Public Affairs, the National Asian Pacific American Legal Consortium, the National Council of La Raza, the Leadership Conference on Civil Rights Education Fund, National Partnership for Women and Families, the Lawyers' Committee for Civil Rights Under Law, and the National Women's Law Center.

A similar delegation will participate in an OSCE meeting in Brussels in September that will examine more broadly racism and discrimination throughout Europe. The Leadership Conference coalition is a model which the European nongovernmental community might well emulate in order for us to be successful in combating antisemitism in Europe – and to work together to fight all forms of racism.

This report examines the situation of antisemitism in Europe since mid-2002, when *Fire and Broken Glass* was first published, the response by governments and the international community to the threat of ongoing violence, and the need for still greater action to address this continuing human rights crisis.

Michael Posner
Executive Director
April 2004

# Executive Summary

*Antisemitism in Europe: Challenging Official Indifference* documents the ongoing scourge of anti-Jewish violence in Europe and the status of efforts by national governments and other institutions to respond to this continuing "violation of human rights." This report updates our 2002 report on antisemitic violence in Europe, *Fire and Broken Glass*, detailing incidents over the two years since that report. It finds that, even as some European governments have taken significant steps to improve their understanding of, and responses to, antisemitic violence and intimidation, there remains what the Foreword to this report terms "a pattern of official indifference" to this serious problem.

A particular focus of this report is the quality of **monitoring and reporting** of antisemitic violence in Europe. The report explains the importance of collecting and disseminating information on such violence in a timely, thorough manner – in order to then develop the means to combat it more effectively.

In addition, we document the continuing failure of some European governments to ensure that existing laws are

**enforced** adequately, and, where necessary, strengthened, to combat continuing antisemitic violence. This includes the need for effective legislation to prosecute and punish hate crimes and provisions to make racist motivation an aggravating circumstance in criminal prosecutions.

As the Foreword notes, "Better documentation alone, of course, will accomplish little if governmental authorities do not strengthen their laws barring such crimes, and investigate and prosecute those who are responsible." Initiatives by Belgium and France in this regard are welcomed. At the same time, improved monitoring and reporting is a critical first step – without which little else is likely to be achieved.

Despite some improvements since the release of *Fire and Broken Glass*, we find that too often antisemitic violence **remains underreported** – what we term "the hate crime information deficit." Most European governments do not provide even basic reporting on the crimes that force many in Europe's Jewish communities to live in fear, and a minority have established national specialized bodies to monitor and address racism. Provisions to ensure there is timely, accurate, and public information on racist violence "is an essential first step in developing effective action to suppress it." This requires government action to make it possible to compile disaggregated data concerning incidents involving every community under threat.

In addition, often when such violence is reported it is linked to antipathy between Jews and Muslims relating to the conflict in the Middle East. As such, what we term the "information deficit" on antisemitism involves both the quantity of information collected on such violence, and the quality of it – meaning the way it which the violence is analyzed and characterized in public statements by government officials.

While it focuses on continuing shortcomings in both law and policy, the report also details a number of **positive developments** over the past two years – reflecting improved policies and practices at the national level in France, Germany, and other countries, as well as work by regional institutions, including the European Commission and the Organization for Security and Cooperation in Europe (OSCE). We issue the report on the eve of an important OSCE antisemitism conference in Berlin, in which we are participating as part of a delegation of U.S.-based non-governmental organizations.

Like our previous report, *Antisemitism in Europe: Challenging Official Indifference* utilizes **international human rights standards** as the framework for discussion of both the violence itself and the status of the government responses. The report reaffirms that antisemitism is "antisemitism is a form of racism and religious intolerance" and "a violation of human rights." As such, the "official indifference" cited in the report's title reflects not only bad policy, but a failure of governments to abide by their own international legal obligations.

We note in this regard that the derogation extends beyond national governments alone to inadequate attention from many **nongovernmental organizations**. For too long, concerns about antisemitic violence have been largely the preserve of Jewish organizations, while much of the human rights community has not treated the issue as a priority warranting urgent attention and a strong response. With *Fire and Broken Glass* and now this report, we are working to change that. We take encouragement in this regard from our own participation in a highly diverse nongovernmental delegation to the OSCE antisemitism conference in Berlin.

As it examines antisemitism through a human rights prism, the report also confronts what has been called the **"new antisemitism."** We show that attacks on Jewish individuals and institutions in Europe have been perpetrated both by extremist rightwing organizations and by members of immigrant Muslim communities who invoke the Middle East conflict in generalized attacks on Jews – treating the victims as what we term "proxy enemies" for the State of Israel.

At the same time, the report emphasizes that European governments and other institutions need to step up efforts to ensure that the fight against antisemitism does not in turn create an environment in which Muslim communities in Europe face increased discrimination and racist violence. The report warns that "antisemitism is often wrongly portrayed as a conflict between minorities, and so a lesser responsibility of European government and society" – and that this may embolden those extremists who are prepared to direct their racism against both Jews and Muslims.

In assessing the debate on the "new antisemitism" we state that while criticism of Israel or the Zionist movement should not be considered inherently antisemitic, when this "disparages or demonizes Jews as individuals or collectively" it crosses the line to become antisemitism.

Finally, having documented the scope of the continuing problem and shortcomings of the responses to it, the report sets out **recommendations** essential for developing and sustaining a more effective approach to combating antisemitic violence. These include recommendations directed at national governments on data collection and reporting, legislation punishing hate crimes, and provisions to consider racist motivation an aggravating circumstance in crimes.

Recommendations also are directed to institutions like the OSCE – beginning with the opportunities afforded by the historic meeting in Berlin. With regard to the latter, we call on OSCE members to issue a strong concluding statement that identifies the effort to fight all forms of antisemitism as a high priority, and specifically assigns responsibility within the OSCE for monitoring and reporting to the Office of Democratic Institutions and Human Rights. Finally, we urge that European governments provide adequate resources to this office to carry out this work effectively.

Building from this second major report, Human Rights First will continue to engage in its own monitoring and reporting that assesses whether European governments and others are living up to any new commitments to improve the reporting of, and responses to, antisemitic violence across much of the continent.

# Introduction

The litany of antisemitic attacks in Europe over the past 18 months is long. Synagogues have been splattered with racist slogans, fire-bombed, and shattered with high explosives; Jewish cemeteries and Holocaust memorials have been desecrated; Jewish schools have been ransacked and set alight.

The November 15, 2003 bombings of two synagogues in Turkey, a member of the Council of Europe, shocked the world and shook that country's small Jewish community. The blasts killed 24 people and wounded at least 300.[1] In France, there were at least two arson attacks on synagogues in 2003,[2] and more recently, on the night of March 22, 2004, a Molotov cocktail was thrown at a Jewish community center in Toulon that houses a synagogue.[3]

Jewish schools and students have also been targeted. In the Jewish community in Uccle, Belgium, the Gan Hai day-care center was ransacked, on July 9, 2003, with excrement thrown against windows and posters written in Hebrew.[4] A pre-dawn arson attack on the Merkaz HaTorah Jewish school in Gagny, a suburb of Paris, France on November 15, 2003, destroyed a large part of the building.

(President Jacques Chirac responded to the attack with a ringing pronouncement that "When a Jew is attacked in France, it is an attack on the whole of France.")

Some atrocities were stopped through effective police action. On June 6, 2003, a man tried to blow up a car, packed with canisters of gas, in front of a synagogue on rue de la Boucheterre in Charleroi, Belgium; the blast was averted and the man arrested.[5] A year earlier, on April 22, 2002, up to 18 gunshots were fired at another synagogue in Charleroi.[6]

Marinus Schöberl, a 16-year-old boy with serious learning disabilities, was brutally tortured and killed on July 12, 2002 in Potzlow by three young assailants who used antisemitic language during the assault. "Say you're a Jew," they reportedly said (he was not) and then repeatedly kicked and beat him. They then dragged him to an abandoned farm where they beat his head repeatedly against a stone pig trough. His body, which had been buried in a cesspit, was found in November 2002. Schöberl's murderers, members of a right-wing organization, later reportedly confessed to the crime.*

* "Neo-Nazis admit killing," Frankfurter Allgemeine Zeitung, May 30, 2003, http://www.faz.com (accessed March 15, 2004); Fekete, Liz, "Youth killed because they thought he was Jewish," IRR News, February 1, 2003 at www.irr.org.uk/cgi-bin/news/open.pl?id=5453 (accessed March 15, 2004).

On October 17, 2003, Rabbi Michel Serfaty was attacked while with his 16-year-old son on the way to the synagogue in Ris-Orangis, a small town outside of Paris. He was harangued with racist epithets – and threats invoking the Middle East – by a group of men in a car. When he leaned down to talk to them, the car door was smashed into his face, knocking him unconscious and bloodying his face. He later told a reporter "What I saw written on their face was hostility and rage."*

* Two arrests were made. "Europe grapples with rising anti-Semitism; Attacks, especially in France, seen tied to Mideast politics," MSNBC News, January 19, 2004, available at http://msnbc.msn.com/id/3999299/ (accessed April 12, 2004). The attackers reportedly shouted slogans calling for "revenge" for the treatment of Palestinians. Initial reports said Rabbi Serfaty was pushed and punched in the face. "French rabbi attacked in street," BBC News, October 19, 2003, available at http://news.bbc.co.uk/2/hi/europe/3205330.stm (accessed April 12, 2004).

In Germany in September 2003 police made arrests in a reported plot to explode a bomb on November 9, the anniversary of the 1938 pogrom known as Kristallnacht, the terrible "Night of Broken Glass." The target was the cornerstone-laying ceremony for a new synagogue in central Munich which hundreds of senior political leaders and members of the Jewish community were expected to attend.[7]

Jews and Jewish sites were also under attack in Russia and elsewhere in the former Soviet Union. A grenade was thrown at a synagogue in Derbent on January 25, 2004, and three Molotov cocktails were thrown at a synagogue in Chelyabinsko on February 4, 2004.[8] On April 12, 2004, a synagogue in Nizhny Novgorod was attacked.[9] Arsonists attempted to set fire to a synagogue in Minsk, Belarus, on August 27, 2003 by dousing the doorway with kerosene. The façade of the building was damaged in this fifth arson attempt there in two years.[10]

# Antisemitism in Europe:
## Challenging Official Indifference

### A Pattern of Intimidation and Violence

The continuing violence of 2003 and early 2004 largely follows a pattern set in 2002, a watershed year for antisemitic violence in Europe. Many countries then saw an increase in attacks on individuals because they are Jewish or thought to be Jewish as well as on community sites such as synagogues, Jewish community centers, and shops. Jewish cemeteries and Holocaust memorials were desecrated and severely damaged. Such incidents were reported across much of Europe.

A record of attacks on Jews by Europeans and immigrants who invoke the Middle East conflict when demonizing Jews has been a part of this picture of antisemitism. So too are threats and attacks by organized political movements of the extreme right, including long-standing neo-nazi movements in Western Europe and ultra-nationalist movements in the Russian Federation. Attacks by racist "skinheads" continue to be a common feature of antisemitic violence.

Attacks that are directly tied to the Middle East conflict are a further part of this panorama – the synagogue bombings in Istanbul in November 2003 exemplified this violence. In these attacks, organized political groups launched terrible attacks on Jewish sites, targeting Jews as such for racist attacks as if proxy enemies in their conflicts with Israel.

Evidence from Spanish police that the perpetrators of the train bombings in Madrid in March 2004 had considered bombing a Jewish community center appeared further to reflect a new dimension to antisemitic violence in Europe.[11] In the wake of the Istanbul bombings, there seems little doubt that organized political groups pose a continuing threat of racist attacks on Jews to give voice to their enmity with Israel. Generalized fear of terrorism, in turn, risks exacerbating xenophobia and discrimination against Europe's Muslim population.

These concerns mean that in the fight against antisemitism we must firmly counter any tendency toward a generalized condemnation of Europe's large Muslim population as complicit in antisemitic violence. This concern is particularly acute in the context of rampant anti-Muslim and anti-immigrant violence in Europe since the September 2001 attacks on the United States. In this context of fear and polarization, strenuous efforts are required to prevent the fight against discrimination and racist violence against Jews in Europe from bringing new forms of discrimination in its wake. These issues are considered further below in a discussion of the concept of a "new antisemitism."

Increasingly, both perpetrators and victims are young people. Overall, 50 percent of all 2003 incidents recorded by the Representative Council of Jewish Institutions of France (Conseil Représentatif des Institutions Juives de France, CRIF), a nongovernmental organization, were directed against Jewish young people.[12] In incident reports, in turn, the attackers are often described as groups of young people.

There are numerous examples in community-based monitoring reports. In Berlin, a group of youths attacked a 19-year-old Orthodox Jew visiting from the U.S. as he left the subway on May 14, 2003. According to his account, they threw fruit at him and asked if he was Jewish; when the young man didn't answer, they beat him.[13] Scores of similar incidents, involving groups of young people attacking visibly Jewish individuals, often while using public transport, were also reported in France.[14]

An alarming level of both verbal and physical abuse was reported against Jewish students in and around schools in both 2002 and 2003.[15] On April 10, 2002, attackers reportedly threw stones at a school bus of the Lubavitch Gan Menahem Jewish school in Paris as students were boarding; one student was injured. On May 16, 2003, a Jewish schoolgirl from the Longchamp School in Marseille was reportedly attacked and verbally abused by a group of ten girls from a nearby school.[16] In Denmark, a group of four or five attackers kicked and beat a 15-year-old student of a Danish Jewish school in November 2003; in September and October, there were reports of youths spitting on, insulting, and threatening children at the same school.[17]

On September 21, 2003, a Russian teenager was reportedly seriously injured when he approached an antisemitic poster that was wired with explosives at a Kaliningrad playground.[18] On September 2, according to RIA-Novosti news service, an antisemitic sign with a device with wires sticking out of it was found.[19] In 2002, there were 18 reported instances in Russia of booby traps attached to antisemitic posters and planted by roadways or in public places.[20]

The desecration of religious sites, cemeteries, and memorials was reported across a wide swath of Europe and formed a part of the threatening environment of antisemitism. The Community Security Trust (CST) recorded seven Jewish cemetery desecrations in the United Kingdom in 2003, including the defacing of hundreds of graves at the Plashet cemetery in West Ham, London in May, the largest single such incident in British history. CST also reported that 22 synagogues in the U.K. were desecrated in 2003, while 18 were in some way attacked in 2002. [21]

In Greece, "Death to Jews" was scrawled on the Holocaust memorial in the Ioannina Jewish cemetery in October 2003 (graves in this cemetery were previously desecrated in April 2002), and the Thessalonica Holocaust Monument was defaced in February 2003 for the second time. The newly inaugurated Holocaust monument on the island of Rhodes was desecrated on June 23, 2002.[22]

In Germany, at least three Jewish cemeteries (in Beeskow, Gundesberg, and Kassel) were desecrated and four Holocaust memorials defaced (in Berlin, Ravensbruck, and Saxony-Anhalt) between July and November 2003.[23]

Cemeteries in Eastern Europe were also desecrated in 2003. Vandals attacked graves in Jewish cemeteries in Humenne (November 19), Nove Mesto nad Vahom

(October 20-26) and Banovce nad Bedravou (January 21) in Slovakia.[24] On November 10, 2003 groundskeepers discovered defaced tombstones in the Jewish cemetery in Trutnov, Czech Republic. The stones had been kicked over and broken off at the base.[25] In Latvia, the local press reported on September 13, 2003, that vandals had overturned more than 20 gravestones in the Bikernieki Forest Cemetery in Riga and defaced others with Nazi slogans and swastikas.[26]

In Russia, tombstones and graves were destroyed in 2003 in the Jewish cemeteries of Pyatigorsk (June 28) and Makhachkala (April 2).[27] Most recently, roughly 50 gravestones were vandalized with swastikas and anti-Jewish graffiti in the Jewish cemetery of St. Petersburg in February 2004.[28]

These were some of the most resonant manifestations of antisemitic violence. They are representative of hundreds of other attacks on people and property that have not been recorded by governments or made public by nongovernmental monitors – much less making the headlines. Jewish communities in countries throughout Europe are witnessing a continuing spiral of antisemitic violence and living in a climate of fear.

## Responding to Antisemitism

Threats and attacks on Jews and Jewish institutions have continued at a high level since mid-2002, when Human Rights First published *Fire and Broken Glass*. But since then, some national governments and multilateral institutions have paid greater attention to the rise of antisemitism. The media on both sides of the Atlantic have focused on the issue to a greater extent. This section concerns the role of inter-governmental institutions in addressing antisemitism in Europe. National initiatives are set out in a separate country-by-country section further below.

European institutions created to address racism and xenophobia, such as the Council of Europe's European Commission against Racism and Intolerance (ECRI) and the European Union's European Monitoring Centre on Racism and Xenophobia (EUMC), have all placed antisemitism higher on the agenda.

Unlike the Council of Europe and the European Union (), the Organization for Security and Cooperation in Europe (OSCE), whose 55 members include all of Europe and Canada and the United States, has no special body to address racism. This notwithstanding, progress has been made toward its placing antisemitism – and other forms of racism – on its agenda. This is discussed further below.

Despite the increased attention to antisemitism by European institutions, there has been insufficient progress in monitoring and reporting on antisemitism at the national level, serious problems with record-keeping practices and systems of redress remain, and high levels of anti-Jewish threats and violence continue across the region. And while most European governments now have strong laws in place criminalizing antisemitic and other racist violence, investigations and prosecutions of specific crimes often are not pursued. This combination of inadequate data collection and gaps in law enforcement create a climate where further acts of antisemitic violence are inevitable.

## Inter-Governmental Initiatives

In our 2002 report, we noted among other major problems the lack of official recognition of the gravity of the problem of antisemitism. Since then, some progress has been made. Belated but welcome statements and initiatives, both at the national and European level, have served to acknowledge the severity of the problem and to place the issue of antisemitism higher on the agenda.

On March 31, 2004, the European Monitoring Centre on Racism and Xenophobia (EUMC) published a 345-page report on antisemitism in the 15 member states of the European Union (). The report, which is discussed further below, is the first such investigative report officially published by the center, and the first report produced using information from the European Union's nascent antiracism monitoring network, RAXEN – the Reseau européen d'information sur le racisme et la xenophobie (European Information Network on Racism and Xenophobia).

The report incorporates information on the 15 member states compiled by RAXEN's National Focal Points, which it described as "mainly 'consortia' between research organisations, specialised bodies and NGOs." Although the report sets out to cover 2002 and 2003, most of the National Focal Points provided information based largely on monitoring for the period May 15 to June 15, 2002 only – the terms of reference of an earlier study commissioned by EUMC. Significant updated data and analysis beyond this temporal snapshot is uneven. The report also includes a report on "Perceptions of Antisemitism in Europe."

The European Commission against Racism and Intolerance (ECRI), a Council of Europe body, has also taken up the issue of antisemitism: the institute is currently drafting a general policy recommendation on antisemitism that should be adopted at the organization's plenary session in June 2004. The draft will be circulated among relevant NGOs for comment before its adoption.

The OSCE's unprecedented conference on antisemitism, held in June 2003 in Vienna, Austria, had no decision-making powers, but was notable as a high-level acknowledgement of the problem of antisemitism. The conference brought more than 400 delegates from member governments and nongovernmental organizations.

Conference delegates offered support for immediate action by OSCE members and institutions to better monitor and report upon antisemitic acts. This was a needed response to what Human Rights First called a "see no evil, hear no evil" information deficit within the OSCE's own human rights mechanisms and in the governments of many European states.

In a statement to the conference, Human Rights First joined with other human rights groups to urge that the conference represent only the beginning of a sustained effort on the part of states and the OSCE as an institution: "to monitor and combat discrimination and violence faced by Jewish communities throughout the OSCE region."

Delegates to the OSCE's Vienna Conference agreed to reaffirm commitments made in Copenhagen in 1990 (the "Copenhagen Declaration") to condemn racial and ethnic hatred, including antisemitism, and to undertake effective follow-up action to demonstrate these commitments in practice.[29]

On April 28-29, 2004, the OSCE will hold a follow-up meeting in Berlin of even greater importance. Its agenda will cover best practices to prevent antisemitism through awareness-raising, education, the rule of law and anti-discrimination legislation, law enforcement, cultural preservation, and methodologies for combating antisemitism. OSCE governments are expected to commit to formal mechanisms to monitor and act against antisemitism on an ongoing basis. This will be followed on September 13-14, 2004, in Brussels, by the OSCE's Conference on Tolerance and the Fight against Racism, Xenophobia and Discrimination, which will tackle a broader agenda to address racism and discrimination in Europe.

Although the Vienna meeting was solely consultative in nature, the OSCE's governing body, the Council of Ministers, took up the issue of antisemitism and the Vienna recommendations at its December 2003 meeting in Maastricht. Its resolutions included calls for increased monitoring and reporting. The council's Decision No. 4/03, on "Tolerance and Non-Discrimination":

> Encourages all participating States to collect and keep records on reliable information and statistics on hate crimes, including on forms of violent manifestations of racism, xenophobia, discrimination, and antisemitism, as discussed and recommended [at Vienna]. Recognizing the importance of legislation to combat hate crimes, participating States will inform the ODIHR about existing legislation regarding crimes fuelled by intolerance and discrimination, and,

where appropriate, seek the ODIHR's assistance in the drafting and review of such legislation...[30]

A further decision, moreover, for the first time assigns the OSCE's Warsaw-based Office of Democratic Institutions and Human Rights (ODIHR) an express role in monitoring and combating antisemitism and other forms of racism, in collaboration with other regional antiracism bodies and nongovernmental organizations. The OSCE now also requires ODIHR to report on its activities in this regard:

Tasks the ODIHR, in full co-operation, *inter alia*, with the United Nations Committee on the Elimination of Racial Discrimination (UNCERD), the European Commission against Racism and Intolerance (ECRI) and the European Monitoring Center on Racism and Xenophobia (EUMC), as well as relevant NGOs, with serving as a collection point for information and statistics collected by participating States, and with reporting regularly on these issues, including in the format of the Human Dimension Implementation Meeting, as a basis for deciding on priorities for future work. The ODIHR will, *inter alia*, promote best practices and disseminate lessons learned in the fight against intolerance and discrimination.[31]

In the context of the Maastricht decisions, ODIHR has launched a project called "Tolerance and Non-Discrimination" with the stated objectives of strengthening ODIHR's response to racism, xenophobia, and antisemitism and to increase compliance with OSCE commitments and other international standards on tolerance and non-discrimination. In addition to a few educational initiatives already underway, the project, while severely under-funded, has to-date launched a comparative study of the monitoring and reporting methodologies of ECRI, EUMC, and the European Union's committee on the International Convention on the Elimination of All Forms of Racial Discrimination (CERD) to identify what ODIHR's value-added contribution in this field could be.[32] As ODIHR builds up its expertise in this area, an important first task could be monitoring and reporting on those countries outside of the Council of Europe and the – Belarus and the Central Asian states – that do not fall under the purview of either ECRI or EUMC.

The European Commission held its own two-day seminar on antisemitism in February 2004. The conference was co-organized with the European Jewish Congress and the Conference of European Rabbis. In his opening remarks, President of the European Commissioner Romano Prodi recognized what he called "vestiges of the historical antisemitism that was once widespread in Europe" and "another context in which a form of antisemitism may develop and which feeds on the unresolved conflict in the Middle East." He concluded that "whatever form antisemitism may take, a constant policy concern of ours must be to banish all such manifestations from the Union."[33] The seminar was again welcomed by Jewish activists as a high-level recognition of the problem. While many proposals on the preventive and legislative level were presented, no specific decisions were taken.

Leaders of the United Nations, too, have also focused attention on the severity of the threat of antisemitism. In a January 13, 2004 speech on intolerance and discrimination, U.N. Secretary-General Kofi Annan addressed the persistence of prejudice and discrimination around the world.[34] After addressing the increased "suspicion, harassment, and discrimination" against

Muslims, particularly in the West, he addressed the rise of antisemitism: "Another dangerous hatred blights our world: antisemitism." This, he said, added new chapters to "the long history of persecution, pogroms, institutionalized discrimination and other degradation, culminating in the Holocaust, that has been inflicted on the Jews." He stressed that the phenomenon was both old and new:

> Yet new wrongs are heaped upon old: by those who seek to deny the fact of the Holocaust or its uniqueness, and by those who continue to spread lies and vile stereotypes about Jews and Judaism. The recent upsurge of attacks on Jews, synagogues, cemeteries and other Jewish targets in Europe, Turkey and elsewhere show this hatred to be not just the stuff of history, but virulent still.

## Monitoring and Reporting on Antisemitism – The Information Deficit Continues

Though welcome, European-level initiatives to address antisemitism are no substitute for concrete national action to improve monitoring mechanisms, record-keeping, and effective systems of redress. Both the European Commission against Racism and Intolerance (ECRI) and the European Monitoring Centre on Racism and Xenophobia (EUMC) have consistently noted the lack of consistent, transparent and uniform monitoring and reporting practices on racism in many of the 45 countries in the Council of Europe (which includes all of the European Union (E.U.) member states and much of the OSCE's membership).

In its Annual Report 2002, the EUMC urged all member states to "install a reporting and monitoring system for racist crimes that is clear, consistent and accessible; maintain statistics on the treatment of racist crimes in the criminal justice system, from the police to the courts; ensure that monitoring categories for victims are disaggregated by race and religion; and publish annual reports on racist crimes."[35] In its country-by-country reports, ECRI is often obliged to encourage authorities to introduce coherent and comprehensive systems for data collection on minority groups.[36] Monitoring and reporting on antisemitism is particularly deficient, revealing that many countries have failed to follow ECRI's country specific recommendations and EUMC's general recommendations on improving data collection and reporting on racist crimes.

The EUMC published its report "Manifestations of Antisemitism in the 2002-2003" on March 31, 2004. The report analyzes in detail the shortcomings in monitoring and reporting on antisemitism in the 15 nations, noting the "great differences between countries in the quality and quantity of the data."[37] The EUMC reports draws some stark country-by-country conclusions in its comments on the sources of data: [38]

- Austria has "no specialised body to record incidents, and a lack of consistency in recording complaints of racial discrimination in general and antisemitism in particular."

- Belgium, "in the absence of any official systematic monitoring," is covered only through nongovernmental sources."

- In Denmark, police record racist crimes without disaggregating by category, so that antisemitic crimes remain largely invisible in official statistics.

The majority of governments – Austria, Belgium, Greece, Spain, Ireland, Luxembourg, Italy, Portugal and Finland – conduct no systematic monitoring of antisemitic incidents at all.[39]

On the other end of the spectrum, Germany, France, The Netherlands, Sweden, and the United Kingdom do collect and publish reliable official or semi-official data on antisemitism:[40]

- France: "official data and information are analysed and published by the French Human Rights Commission."

- Germany: the Federal Ministry of the Interior and Federal Ministry of Justice produced relevant information, with data recorded on "extreme right wing and antisemitic offences."

- Netherlands: statistics are provided by "official bodies, NGOs and research organizations." Statistics on incidents in 2003, however, were unavailable for the EUMC's 2004 report.

- Sweden: "a formal record of antisemitic incidents" is provided yearly by the police.

- United Kingdom: "statistics are provided by the Metropolitan police, and for the rest of the country by an independent Jewish organisation." But only the Metropolitan Police for Greater London disaggregate data on antisemitism; the police in Manchester and Leeds, two other cities with a significant Jewish population, are expected to introduce this practice in the near future.[41]

## Country-by-Country Legislation and Monitoring Standards[42]

|  | Monitoring Practices |
|---|---|
| Austria | No systematic monitoring – no specialized body to record incidents |
| Belgium | No systematic monitoring – no systematic official monitoring |
| Denmark | Racist crimes recorded by police but no disaggregation by category |
| Finland | No systematic monitoring |
| France | Reliable data collected and published by the French Human Rights Commission |
| Greece | No systematic monitoring |
| Ireland | No systematic monitoring |
| Italy | No systematic monitoring |
| Luxembourg | No systematic monitoring |
| Netherlands | Reliable data collected and published by official bodies, NGOs, and research organizations |
| Portugal | No systematic monitoring |
| Spain | No systematic monitoring |
| Sweden | Reliable data collected and published by the police |
| United Kingdom | Reliable data collected and published by the police (London) and by an independent Jewish organization (rest of country) |

In the absence of systematic government monitoring, nongovernmental and Jewish community organizations gather the only available case information and statistics. Methodology, categorization of incidents, and procedures for confirmation tend to vary widely among these organizations and between countries, so meaningful comparisons are difficult.

The lack of systematic data collection can offer a dangerously misleading picture of antisemitism. While increasingly effective monitoring and reporting in countries like Germany and France now reveal high levels of antisemitic violence, high levels of anti-Jewish violence may also be present but largely unrecognized in countries where little or no data is collected. EUMC cautions that while some countries do indeed appear to have low levels of antisemitic incidents, in others "it is clear that it is rather the official denial of the phenomenon of antisemitism than the absence of it that has led to the refusal to collect data systematically."[43]

Even where guidelines exist for recording antisemitic incidents as such, the EUMC found that police do not always properly record complaints received, either because the guidelines themselves are ambiguous or because of inadequate training and awareness within the police force.[44] In addition, not all antisemitic incidents are reported to authorities; victims often choose either to refrain from reporting or place their complaint to victim hotlines operated by nongovernmental organizations. This problem of under-reporting is compounded by over-reporting, in cases where unofficial bodies collecting data do not have rigorous validation methodologies and where different agencies – governmental and nongovernmental –

collecting data do not have a sufficient level of cooperation to avoid multiple counts of the same incidents.[45]

In a few countries, such as France and the United Kingdom, official bodies and community-based NGOs appear to have established a good level of cooperation and their respective data on antisemitic incidents tend to match and confirm one another, providing a reliable picture of the phenomenon. Indeed, EUMC notes that "the 'optimal' structure of bodies within a monitoring area, ensuring, as far as possible, the most comprehensive and valid results, is the combination of a central official monitoring facility with one or more NGOs (operating, for example, victim hotlines), mutually complimenting and examining each other."[46]

In its General Policy Recommendations No. 2, adopted in June 1997 and No. 7, adopted in December 2002, ECRI called on all member states to institute independent national specialized bodies to monitor racism and racial discrimination, including antisemitism. These bodies should be tasked with providing assistance to victims, investigation powers, the right to initiate and participate in court proceedings, monitoring legislation and providing advice to legislative and executive authorities, as well as awareness-raising of issues around racism and racial discrimination.[47] To date, only 16 countries within the Council of Europe have some kind of specialized body; of these, only the entities in the United Kingdom, The Netherlands, and Sweden have the kind of extensive functions proposed by ECRI.[48]

## Compliance with European Union Directive to Create a Specialized National Antiracism Body

|  | Compliance with European Union Directive to Create a Specialized Antiracism Body[49] | Functioning specialized bodies of some kind |
|---|---|---|
| Austria | No | [Legislation pending] |
| Belgium | No | Yes |
| Denmark | Yes |  |
| Luxembourg | No | [Legislation adopted, but reportedly not functioning] |
| Finland | No | Yes |
| France | Yes |  |
| Germany | No | [Legislation pending] |
| Greece | No | [Legislation pending] |
| Ireland | No | Yes |
| Italy | Yes | Legislation adopted, but reportedly not functioning] |
| Netherlands | No | Yes |
| Portugal | No | Yes |
| Spain | No | Legislation adopted, but reportedly not functioning] |
| Sweden | Yes |  |
| United Kingdom | Yes |  |

ECRI policy recommendations provide useful guidelines but they are not binding on the 45 member states of the Council of Europe. However, the 15 members of the , as well as the accession states that will join the  on May 1, 2004, are bound by Council Directive 2000/43/EC, known as the Racial Equality Directive. This directive requires the establishment of a specialized body, though its independence per se is not stipulated.[50] While the deadline for transposition of the directive into national law was July 2003, the majority of countries have yet to adopt the necessary legislation. Indeed, as of January 1, 2004, only five of the 15 current  member states had complied with the transposition requirements (Denmark, France, Italy, Sweden, and United Kingdom).[51]

A corollary problem to insufficient data collection is inadequate legislation on racist crimes. Racist violence is a crime in all countries belonging to the , but a racist motive for a criminal act is an aggravating factor in legislation only in France, Belgium, Germany, Austria, Portugal, Sweden, and the United Kingdom. Belgium introduced a new law in February 2003 that makes racist intent an aggravating circumstance in a wide range of crimes – and which should provide a basis for future reporting on hate crimes.[52] France, too, in an important step, amended its criminal code in February 2003 to make a racist motive an aggravating factor. In accordance with the European Convention on Human Rights, hate speech, racist propaganda, and incitement to hatred or violence are criminal acts in all  states. The European Commission against Racism and Intolerance (ECRI) has noted that "The persistence of racial discrimination…is closely linked to the lack of effective anti-discrimination legislative provisions in most member States…This problem is compounded by the unsatisfactory implementation of existing anti-racist provisions..."[53]

## Compliance with Recommendations to Make Racist Intent an Aggravating Circumstance to be Taken Into Account in Criminal Prosecutions

|  | Racist motivation is an aggravating factor in crime |
|---|---|
| Austria | Yes |
| Belgium | Yes, since 2003. |
| Denmark | Yes |
| Ireland | No |
| Italy | Yes |
| Finland | No |
| France | Yes, since 2003. |
| Germany | Yes |
| Greece | No |
| Luxembourg | No |
| Netherlands | No |
| Portugal | Yes |
| Spain | No |
| Sweden | Yes |
| United Kingdom | Yes |

In November 2001, the European Commission presented a proposal for a Framework Decision on Combating Racism and Xenophobia. Framework Decisions are employed to encourage comparable approximation of laws and regulations among member states on criminal matters. The draft Framework Decision on racism and xenophobia sets out in broad terms the obligation to criminalize racist and xenophobic conduct by individuals, groups and legal entities.[54]

The proposal has languished since it was first introduced in November 2001. President of the European Commission Romano Prodi took the opportunity of the Commission's seminar on antisemitism in February 2004 to publicly urge the Council to adopt the measure as quickly as possible. ECRI's December 2002 General Policy Recommendation No. 7 on national legislation to combat racism and racial discrimination also addresses this issue; it contains broadly similar provisions to those in the proposed Framework Decision. As noted above, ECRI's recommendations are considered important guidelines but are not binding on the 45 member states of the Council of Europe.

# A Country by Country Snapshot

Information on a sample of European countries with continuing reports of antisemitic violence follow below. The sources include the antiracism bodies of the European Union and the Council of Europe, nongovernmental human rights reporting, bulletins from Jewish organizations that monitor and report on antisemitism, and the media. The account is inevitably incomplete, as one common finding throughout the region is that monitoring and reporting remains inadequate.

# Austria

In Austria, the European Monitoring Centre on Racism and Xenophobia (EUMC) contrasted the low numbers of antisemitic incidents reported by the Federal Ministry of the Interior, which covers antisemitism under its annual reports on "right-wing extremism," and the reports of the nongovernmental Forum gegen Antisemitismus. The latter cited 108 incidents of antisemitism in 2003, a significant rise over 2002. These included damage to synagogues, vandalism to cemeteries, a bomb threat to a Jewish school, and several serious assaults, including the following:

- On February 10, 2003, four "skinheads" reportedly harassed a man on the Vienna subway by shouting "Heil Hitler" and flourishing a neo-nazi poster in his face, then beat the man with a belt. Although other passengers reportedly did not intervene, police arrived, arrested the alleged perpetrators, and registered the complaint. Court proceedings were reportedly pending.

- On May 10, 2003, skinheads kicked and threw beer on a rabbi; two shopkeepers assisted in detaining the two assailants pending the arrival of police; the two were reportedly interviewed by police but then released.

- In July 2003, an Orthodox Jew was reportedly beaten unconscious in a racist attack in Vienna.[55]

- On July 1, 2003, a Jewish family was reportedly refused entrance to a restaurant by its Muslim owners and then "in the ensuing brawl," members of the family were beaten by customers. Police reportedly responded and took statements from all parties.[56]

# Belgium

In Belgium, attacks on individuals and institutions continued, while despite promising new legislation the government still failed to monitor or report on racist violence (see below). On March 18, 2003, unidentified attackers firebombed a synagogue in the Anderlecht district of Brussels district, damaging its entry[57] – a year before, a synagogue there had been badly damaged by two firebombs and Jewish shops had been daubed with slogans declaring "Death to the Jews." The failed attack on a synagogue in Charleroi, Belgium in June 2003 has already been cited.

The EUMC's 2004 report on antisemitism notes that, notwithstanding past criticism, Belgium still "does not have an official monitoring system for antisemitism,"[58] a failing identified in *Fire and Broken* Glass. The report draws upon information from the Centre for Equal Opportunities and Opposition to Racism (CEOOR), which served as the National Focal Point within the EUMC's antiracism network, and reported having received 30 complaints relating to antisemitism in 2002 and another 30 in 2003. It said nongovernmental sources had reported one incident of extreme violence, five assaults, and four cases of damage and desecration of property.[59] The report also cites information from the nongovernmental Bureau Executif de Surveillance Communautaire (besc), however, which recorded 62 "hostile acts" in 2002; it said 39 acts targeted individuals, while 23 targeted buildings.[60]

The Council of Europe's European Commission against Racism and Intolerance (ecri) released its third report on Belgium in January 2004 (covering the situation up to June 27, 2003), focusing on implementation of recommendations from past reports. ecri described some progress "in the area of monitoring the way in which the criminal justice system deals with acts inspired by racism and xenophobia."[61]

Two laws were adopted in 2003 to address crimes motivated by racism and xenophobia and establish civil remedies against discrimination. These responded to a previous ecri recommendation that provisions in laws be introduced to establish that the racist motivation constitutes a specific aggravating circumstance.[62] The implementation of the new provisions will require careful monitoring, but should provide a basis for future statistical reporting on incidents of racist threats and violence. To this end, the new legislation expressly mandated the official Centre for Equal Opportunities and Opposition to Racism to receive and make public information concerning the fight against racism:

> to collect and publish statistical data and courts' decisions as necessary for the evaluation of the implementation of the laws against racism and discrimination; receive information from the competent authorities on facts which may point at possible breaches of the laws against racism and

discrimination and be informed by the authorities on the follow-up given; receive a yearly communication by the Ministry of Justice of judicial statistics on the implementation of the laws against racism and discrimination and of the relative decisions; be informed by the Comité P or the General Inspection of the federal and local Police of the follow-up given to any situations brought to their attention by the Centre and be informed of any action taken by these institutions at their own initiative, in the fields covered by the Centre.[63]

In response, ECRI further recommends that the resources of the Centre be reviewed with a view to ensuring that it is able to carry out the additional responsibilities. The report called for further concerted efforts to respond to the "increase in manifestations of antisemitism and islamophobia…," while stressing the need to address this "as problems affecting Belgian society as a whole and not only some of its communities."

# Denmark

The EUMC's 2004 report on antisemitism found no reports of what it termed "extreme violence" in Denmark in 2003, but evidence of at least two assaults as well as serious instances of antisemitic hate speech via the Internet which resulted in prosecutions. The authors qualified their findings, however, by stressing that official statistics on "racist" incidents do not make clear "how many incidents within official statistics relate specifically to antisemitism." The report referred to two incidents of physical assaults and one incident of vandalism in 2002, but the coverage appeared to be limited to the period May 15-June 15, 2002, its initial focus period.

The Tel Aviv University Stephen Roth Institute's report on Denmark for 2002-2003 described unprecedented levels of "physical violence, destruction of property, verbal and written threats and harrasment" in 2002, with 65 recorded incidents.[64]

# France

The antisemitic violence that earned France an unwelcome notoriety in 2002 continued in 2003 and early 2004, although some progress was reported. The French government that came to power in the April 2002 elections, under the center-right government of President Jacques Chirac, has taken a more aggressive stance against antisemitism. Security measures were heightened at Jewish institutions almost immediately; in February 2004, then-Interior Minister Nicolas Sarkozy announced that $18.61 million had been earmarked for increased security at Jewish synagogues, schools and offices. He stated that his government is "determined to eradicate antisemitism in this country."[65]

In February 2003, France amended its criminal code to make a racist motive an aggravating factor in punishing crimes.

Following the fire-bombing of the Jewish school in Gagny in November 2003, President Jacques Chirac stated that "When a Jew is attacked in France, it is an attack on the whole of France."[66] Chirac subsequently instituted an inter-ministerial committee, led by Prime Minister Jean-

Pierre Raffarin, to monitor antisemitic acts in France. Since its creation in November 2003, the Committee has met on a monthly basis and has led to the implementation of new policies.

French Education Ministry Luc Ferry, in February 2003, introduced a ten-point action program to address antisemitism and other forms of racism in schools, to include the formation of special school teams to identify and track incidents, tougher penalties for racist behavior, and handbooks for teachers.[67]

CRIF reported a total of 503 antisemitic incidents in 2003. Although this overall figure is slightly lower than the 517 incidents recorded by that organization in 2002, the number of acts of violence actually increased: in 2003, this Jewish community organization registered 100 reported cases of physical assaults, compared to 75 in 2002, and 67 reported cases of vandalism compared to 39 recorded in 2002.[68]

The official National Consultative Commission on Human Rights (Commission Nationale Consultative des Droits de l'Homme, CNCDH), had recorded 193 violent antisemitic incidents in 2002, a six-fold increase over such incidents recorded in 2001.[69]

In its annual report covering 2003, released in April 2004, CNCDH, concluded that the overall level of racist threats and violence had gone down, from 1,313 in 2002, to 817 reports in 2003.[70] The proportion directed at the Jewish community, however, had risen, from 60 percent to 72 percent in 2003. The statistical breakdown for 2003 identified a total of 588 antisemitic acts (down from 932 in 2002), of which 463 constituted threats and 125 were acts of violence: 70 physical assaults, 46 cases of vandalism, and six cases of arson.[71]

In 21 cases of antisemitic attacks recorded by CNCDH in 2003 serious injuries were reported, the highest reported number since 1993; this was the first time a greater number of injuries were attributed to racist attacks against Jews than those involving any other group. Eleven woundings were reported in other forms of racist attack. The commission also cited police statistics on 49 incidents in which Jewish which institutions were damaged or defaced, including attacks on 28 synagogues and five Jewish schools.[72]

For the CNCDH, the arrests are "insufficient": there were only 81 in 2003 (in contrast to 139 in 2002), in which 47 were the perpetrators of antisemitic violence. While more than 80 percent of racist and antisemitic acts were attributed to the extreme right in the 1990s, no more than 18 percent were in 2003. The newspaper *Libération*'s account of the reports notes that 117 incidents "could be imputed to people from poor and disadvantaged neighborhoods," and that the findings "confirm the tie between racist acts and international events, with a peak last spring coinciding with the conflict in Iraq."[73]

The CNCDH report is just one indicator of the severity of threats and violence against the French Jewish community, reflecting only incidents formally reported to French authorities. Another indicator, in addition to the statistics produced by the community-based CRIF, is the actual level of fear expressed by members of the Jewish community. The sense of anxiety is so great among the Jewish community that some in the Jewish community are now taking up the advice from public officials in the past that Jews conceal their Jewishness in public. The measure of concern was reflected in a November 2003 comment on a radio program in which France's chief rabbi Joseph Sitruk reportedly advised Jews to wear baseball caps instead of yarmulkes to avoid anti-Jewish attacks.[74]

# Germany

The German Interior Ministry recorded a total of 1,334 criminal acts of an antisemitic nature in 2002, down from 1,406 acts recorded in 2001. However, the number of violent antisemitic crimes registered increased from 18 in 2001 to 28 in 2002.[75]

In its second report on Germany, published in July 2001, the Council of Europe's antiracism body ECRI recognized the significant efforts made to combat racism, but concluded that there was still a great deal to do:

> However, Germany is a society in which serious incidents of racially motivated violence occur. This means that issues of racism, antisemitism, xenophobia and intolerance are yet to be adequately acknowledged and confronted. The existing legal framework and policy measures have not proven to be sufficient to effectively deal with or solve these problems. Of deep concern are the situation of and attitudes towards those who are considered as "foreigners", insufficient measures of integration and the lack of recognition of the possibility that German identity may also be associated with other forms of identity than the traditional one.[76]

At the time, ECRI expressed concern at an increase in antisemitism and violent attacks on the Jewish community in Germany, citing in particular the desecration of cemeteries and reported bomb attacks aimed at Jews.

The 2001 report on Germany, the last released by ECRI, described "frequent reports of harassment and attacks, some resulting in death, against members of minority groups," and a situation in which minorities "are afraid to appear in public in certain regions of the country." It said the attacks are aimed "at individuals of foreign origin as well as members of the Jewish community," and that those who are visibly members of a minority were particularly susceptible to attack. The report found that these incidents "are mainly carried out by neo-nazi groups or other extreme right groups, the majority by perpetrators between the ages of fourteen and twenty one. German internal security officials have warned that the German 'hard right' is becoming better armed and more violent."[77]

While the ECRI report stressed the importance of German government measures to combat racist violence through the criminal justice system, it recommended a need for new measures "defining racially motivated offences as specific offences or explicitly providing for racial motivation to be taken into account as an aggravating factor by the courts."[78] The German Penal Code provides for the prosecution of "communication or propaganda" offenses including incitement of hatred or violence against parts of the population, or "against a national, racial, or religious group, or a group defined by national customs and traditions or who abuses, disparages or slanders these groups and thereby attacks human dignity..."[79]

The 2004 report on antisemitism by the European Monitoring Centre on Racism and Xenophobia (EUMC) cited the apparent increase by 69 percent of antisemitic acts from 1999 to 2000, with a further increase reported in 2001. It cited the Interior Ministry figures showing that despite a decrease in the total number of racist offenses, the number of violent antisemitic crimes rose from 18 in 2001 to 28 in 2002. Most of the crimes recorded, however, concerned "incitement and propaganda offenses." Reported incidents included:

- A bottle containing a flammable liquid was thrown at a Berlin synagogue in April 2002, without causing damage.

- A bomb threat was issued on May 28, 2002, related to a call-in show in Frankfurt which hosted by the Vice-chair of the Central Council of Jews in Germany.

- The December 24, 2002 desecration of a Jewish cemetery in Philippsburg, where eight tombstones were broken and 15 were defaced with swastikas.

- The September 2002 desecration of a cemetery in Butzow (Mecklenburg-West Pomerania) where tombstones were sprayed with swastikas and ss markings.

Official statistics for 2003 were unavailable, but the authorities had reportedly recorded 16 violent antisemitic crimes in the first half of the year, with 14 people injured. These included attacks in May 2003 on a 19-year-old Orthodox Jew and another on a 56-year-old man targeted for wearing a Star of David. The report also cited a May 2003 statement by the head of the Central Council of Jews concerning "almost weekly attacks on Jewish cemeteries and Jewish institutions."[80] Incidents continue to be reported from Jewish community organizations.

The Stephen Roth Institute reports a dramatic increase of antisemitic incidents in Berlin, with 255 incidents in 2002 (compared to 106 in 2001 and 56 in 2000). "Jewish students in the capital reportedly hide their Star of David chains and refrain from speaking Hebrew for fear of being attacked," it said.[81]

An example of incidents cited included a threatening letter received in mid-January 2003 by Berlin Rabbi Chaim Rozwaski "which included a packet of ashes and the neo-Nazi slogan 'Lies will become truth - Holocaust II.' Rozowaski, a Holocaust survivor, angered the neo-Nazis by opposing their plan to march through the Jewish quarter of Berlin in 2001."[82]

# Italy

The 2004 EUMC report on Italy, which draws upon Ministry of Interior, nongovernmental organization, and media information, contrasts the high level of what can be termed offensive speech and hate speech in Italy with a low level of actual violence. The National Focal Point review of 2002 "did not find any reports of physical attacks on persons or property" tied to antisemitism, but reported on "verbal threats, anonymous letters, threatening phone calls and graffiti. In 2003, a similar pattern was reported, with a wide range of antisemitic "graffiti, threats and insults, desecration of places and symbols" attributed to "the radical right."

Developments in Italy cited in the EUMC report included the January 2003 sentencing of eight skinheads for criminal conspiracy to commit bodily harm, aggravated by racial motivation: "The group had, over the last years, organised punitive expeditions against their 'enemies', namely Jews, foreigners, policemen and drug dealers."[83] The report also cited a press report of an incident in November 2003 in Padua, in which two students were reportedly threatened and beaten at school by classmates because of their Jewish surname: "Their father, summoned by the school principal, felt compelled to swear that he had been baptized."[84]

In its second report on Italy, made public in April 2002, ECRI notes that Italy has made racist intent an aggravating circumstance in its criminal law: "Section 3 of the Law N° 205/1993 introduces a general aggravating circumstance for all offences committed with a view to discrimination on racial, ethnic, national or religious ground or in order to help organisations with such purposes. The Law also provides that any racially-aggravated offence is prosecuted *ex officio*."[85]

# Latvia

The Council of Europe's antiracism body, ECRI, in its second report on Latvia, noted in 2002 that "[m]anifestations of antisemitism are reportedly not prevalent within Latvian mainstream society and media." At the same time, the report stressed "the absence of reliable data on the situation of minority groups and incidents of discrimination." [86]

Although the information deficit made it difficult to assess the real situation, ECRI registered some antisemitic incidents, "including the bombing of a synagogue, antisemitic inscriptions on Jewish public buildings and desecration of graves. In addition, there have been cases of publication of antisemitic articles in the press." In a widely reported incident, vandals on September 17, 2003, overturned tombstones and sprayed antisemitic graffiti on the walls of Riga's Jewish Cemetery, in an act condemned by national leaders.[87]

ECRI highlighted "[t]he lack of a comprehensive body of anti-discrimination legislation and the need to increase the effectiveness of the criminal law provisions aimed at combating racist and intolerant expressions..." A principal focus of the report was the issue of nationality and language, a dominant issue in many of the successor states of the former Soviet Union where Russian-speakers are among important national minorities.[88]

In its recommendations, in addition to urging a review of the adequacy of legislation "against hate speech and degrading speech," ECRI called upon Latvian authorities "to bring to justice the persons found responsible for … incidents and to closely monitor the situation as concerns manifestations of antisemitism."

The report identified concerns with "Latvian and Russian racist extremist groups, including neo-Nazi groups, and at their activities in Latvia." Activities by these groups which it said required attention included "the publication of racist and antisemitic material, through which exponents of these groups incite to racial hatred and advocate the use of violence, as well as damage to property." ECRI called for "a more vigorous response on the part of the Latvian authorities to the activities of such organizations," while noting that there had been a few cases of prosecutions followed by convictions.

Latvia's 1999 Criminal Code (article 78) prohibits "incitement to national or ethnic hatred or enmity as well as the direct or indirect restriction of economic, political or social rights of - and the direct and indirect creation of privileges for - individuals on the basis of their racial or national origin." But, ECRI adds, the authorities "rarely identify the intention to incite to racial hatred. Very few prosecutions and convictions have been secured under Article 78." [89] Racist motives, in turn, are not considered aggravating circumstances in criminal offenses:

No criminal provisions exist defining ordinary offences with a racist element as specific offences, and there are no provisions explicitly enabling the racist or xenophobic motives of the offender to be taken into account by the courts as an aggravating circumstance when sentencing. In accordance with its general policy recommendation No 1, ECRI encourages the Latvian authorities to introduce such provisions.[90]

Latvia has an independent National Human Rights Office (NHRO), established by law, with a mandate "to educate and inform the general public about human rights; to examine the existing human rights situation and make recommendations on ways to improve it; and to receive and handle individual complaints on alleged human rights violations." The report observes, however, that very few cases of individual complaints connected with racism and discrimination have been addressed.[91]

In accordance with ECRI's general policy recommendation no. 2, it encouraged Latvia to create a specialized body to combat racism and intolerance, or to provide the funds and personnel that would be required for the NHRO to assume this function. This was proposed in the context of a parallel recommendation for adoption "of a comprehensive framework of anti-discrimination legislation." Similarly, in noting the absence of reliable data on the situation of minority groups and incidents of discrimination, ECRI found that "it is necessary to set up a system of data collection and monitoring, in order to uncover and remedy any problems, including differences related to direct or indirect discrimination."[92]

Despite the failure to monitor and report incidents of discriminatory violence, Latvia's laws reportedly require identity documents to give the ethnicity of the bearer – with Jews considered an ethnic group. Passports identify citizens, for example, by ethnicities including Russian, Latvian, or Jewish.[93]

# Netherlands

A nongovernmental organization in the Netherlands recorded 337 antisemitic incidents in 2002, a 140 percent increase over 2001 (including a significant increase in threatening web publications and e-mail); there were 12 incidents of assault and 19 threats of physical violence, up from six and eight, respectively, in 2001.[94]

The EUMC's 2004 report stressed the absence of official information for 2003, while confirming that levels of violence had increased significantly in 2002. The report cites the Dutch Complaints Bureau for Discrimination on the Internet (Meldpunt Discriminatie Internet, MDI), Monitoring Racism and the Extreme Right, a project of the Anne Frank House and Leiden University, the National Federation of Anti-Discrimination Agencies and Hotlines, and the Israel Information and Documentation Center.

The EUMC report contrasts the 46 antisemitic incidents reported in 2002 with the 18 cases reported in 2001, and noted that in 19 of the cases "the perpetrator was believed to be a member of an ethnic minority or there was a clear connection with the Middle East conflict."

The United Nation's Committee on the Elimination of Racial Discrimination, in reviewing the periodic report of the Netherlands on compliance with the Convention on the Elimination of all Forms of Racial Discrimination, expressed concern at the occurrence "of racist and xenophobic incidents, particularly of an anti-Semitic and "islamophobic" nature, and of manifestations of discriminatory attitudes towards ethnic minorities."[95]

# Russian Federation

In Russia, according to international monitors, registered incidents of antisemitic violence and vandalism rose from 37 incidents in 2001 to 73 in 2002.[96] The true number of serious incidents is probably far higher; incident reports from 2003 and early 2004 suggest the level of threats and violence remains high. The Union of Councils for Jews of the Former Soviet Union (known as UCSJ) produces a weekly bulletin that collates information from the Russian news media and nongovernmental monitors, and works closely with human rights groups there. These bulletins regularly report threats and physical assaults on people because they are thought to be Jewish, attacks on synagogues, Jewish cemeteries, and schools, and antisemitic diatribes by nationalist political leaders of Russia's extremist political movements. Some representative incidents follow:

- On December 17, 2003, in the latest of a series of reported attacks on the Kostroma synagogue, a group of young people broke two windows during a service, and daubed antisemitic slogans in and around the building.[97]

- In June, 2003, attackers reportedly broke all of the windows of a synagogue in Yaroslavl, the third attack on that synagogue in two months.[98]

- On election night in Bryansk, December 7, 2003, rocks were reported thrown through two windows of a Jewish school there, the entrance of which was daubed with a swastika and the words "Death to the kikes." Police responded, arresting five youths.[99] On November 29, the newspaper Bryansk regional administration newspaper *Bryansky Rabochy* had run an article criticizing a concert held at the Bryansk synagogue in which the author attributed Russia's economic problems to Jews and described Judaism as linked to "Satan and dark forces."[100]

Antisemitic threats from nationalist political movements in Russia have also included death threats to particular individuals. In July 2003, senior political leaders in Kaliningrad received letters headed "A Tender Proposal to the Kikes of Kaliningrad Oblast and Their Lackeys," which threatened to "physically destroy people of Jewish nationality and their lackeys." According to broadcast reports, the letters, signed in the name of "The Russian Orthodox Warrior Brotherhood," demanded the recipients, most of whom were not Jewish, resign their posts or face reprisals against their families. Regional Duma deputy Solomon Ginzburg told the media this was the fifth wave of threatening letters and graffiti of this kind since early 2001.[101]

In March 2003, the United Nation's Committee on the Elimination of Racial Discrimination reviewed the periodic report of the Russian Federation on its compliance with the Convention on the Elimination of all Forms of Racial Discrimination.[102] The Committee noted the continuing absence of a definition of racial discrimination in domestic legislation, in contravention of article 1 of the convention, and expressed concerns about "the incidence of violent racist attacks against ethnic minorities by, among others, skinheads and neo-Nazis." Similarly, concern was expressed about "reports that racist materials targeting minority groups and perpetuating negative stereotypes are disseminated in the national media." The Committee recommended the government "strengthen its efforts to prevent racist violence and protect members of ethnic minorities and foreigners, including refugees and asylum-seekers."

The CERD Committee expressed particular concern about the political and paramilitary groups known as Cossacks, and the toleration for them by the state:

> While appreciating the particular history of Cossacks in the Russian Federation, the Committee is concerned at reports that some Cossack organizations have engaged in acts of intimidation and violence against ethnic groups. According to information received by the Committee, these organizations, which function as paramilitary units and are used by local authorities to carry out law enforcement functions, enjoy special privileges, including State funding. In this regard, the Committee recommends, in accordance with article 2 (b) of the Convention, that the State party ensure that no support is provided to organizations which promote racial discrimination and that it prevent Cossack paramilitary units from carrying out law enforcement functions against ethnic groups.

Although antisemitism in the Cossack movement has been widely reported, the report does not identify the groups subjected to discriminatory treatment by Cossack groups.

The U.S. Department of State's annual International Religious Freedom Report for 2003 found that "[o]fficial discrimination, vandalism, and occasional violence against Jews continued, although Jewish leaders have stated publicly that the state-sponsored anti-Semitism of the Soviet era no longer exists."

The U.S. Department of State's report followed up to the May 2002 incident in which Moscow resident Tatyana Sapunova was badly injured when trying to remove an antisemitic sign rigged with explosives on a Moscow highway. It said more than 15 similar signs "calling for 'Death to Kikes' and other slogans were discovered…around the country," some rigged with explosives. Two people reportedly died while attempting to remove them. Although Sapunova was awarded the Order of Courage by President Putin, there were no prosecutions for the crime, and the report highlighted a statement by Moscow police spokesman Farid Khasanov, who "referred to one of the mock booby-trapped signs as 'a practical joke.'"[103]

In September 2003, support by the European Union was announced for a joint project by Russian human rights organizations and the Union of Councils for Jews in the Former Soviet Union, "to monitor cases of racism, antisemitism, and ethnic discrimination that have flourished in Russia." The project, which is to deploy monitors in 89 Russian regions, is to involve work by the Moscow Bureau on Human Rights and UCSJ in collaboration with the Moscow Helsinki Group, the Krasnodar-based School of Peace, and government bodies.[104]

# Sweden

Police in Sweden investigated 131 complaints related to antisemitic crimes in 2002, including one case of gross assault (which includes crimes defined as attempted murder or attempted manslaughter) and five assaults, 47 cases of harassment, and 11 instances of vandalism. Jewish community officials believe the actual number of total antisemitic incidents is higher.[105]

# United Kingdom

In the United Kingdom, the Community Security Trust (CST), which defines anti-Semitic incidents as "any malicious act aimed at the Jewish community or Jewish individuals as Jews," recorded 350 antisemitic incidents in 2002, up from 310 in 2001. Of these, 47 were violent physical attacks – 13 percent of the total and an increase of 15 percent over 2001. There were 55 incidents of damage and desecration, covering incidents directed at Jewish property, including synagogues and cemeteries.[106]

In its annual report for 2003, the CST reported 375 antisemitic incidents in Britain in 2003, the second highest number in two decades: "The incidents included 15 violent attacks, one of them on a Midlands rabbi. The assault victims, clearly identifiable Jews, were punched, kicked and spat at. In addition, swastikas and anti-Semitic slogans were painted on Jewish institutions and prominent community members received hate mail."[107] There were a reported 89 antisemitic incidents in the first quarter of 2003, a 75 percent rise over the same period in 2002, coinciding with political debate concerning the United Kingdom's involvement in the Iraq war. CST press spokesmen Michael Whine, in a BBC interview, observed that "The Iraq war fed anti-Semitism, because groups from across the political and social spectrum alleged that the war was fought for 'Zionist' interests."[108] Jews as such were demonized for policies attributed to Israel and the United Kingdom government.

Reports from the United Kingdom also illustrate the way antisemitism represents much more than isolated incidents, especially when particular Jewish individuals are targeted. The London *Daily Telegraph* in February 2004 reported on a 14-month campaign of violence and intimidation waged against the former general secretary of the Labour party, Lord Triesman, which was attributed to a neo-Nazi group called Combat 18. Police reportedly described a series of 12 separate attacks on his London home as driven by antisemitism. Lord Triesman, although described as "not a practising Jew," observed that "When a group like Combat 18 spray swastikas and slogans on your walls and brick your windows, it's evident what it's all about.[109] Gerry Gable, the publisher of an anti-fascist magazine called *Searchlight,* was cited in the same report on the practice of extreme right organizations of "orchestrating campaigns on the internet against prominent Jews by circulating their names and addresses. 'They believe they are participating in a race war,' he said."[110]

# International Standards

International human rights law contains clear provisions barring racial discrimination. The International Covenant on Civil and Political Rights, ICCPR (1966), requires each state party to guarantee those rights to all, "without distinction of any kind, such as race, colour, sex, language, religion, political or other opinion, national or social origin, property, birth or other status" (Article 2). The European Convention on Human Rights (1953) contains a similar obligation (Article 14). The International Convention on the Elimination of All Forms of Racial Discrimination, CERD (1966), defines racism as:

> any distinction, exclusion, restriction or preference based on race, colour, descent, or national origin which has the purpose or effect of nullifying or impairing the recognition, enjoyment or exercise, on an equal footing, of human rights and fundamental freedom in the political, economic, social, cultural or any other field of public life. [Article 1.1]

Antisemitism is racial discrimination under the CERD definition, and the Committee on the Elimination of Racial Discrimination, charged with monitoring implementation of the treaty, has included attention to treatment of Jewish minorities in their examinations of state compliance.[111]

States party to CERD are obligated to condemn and eliminate racial discrimination by both public officials and private individuals. The authoritative interpretations of the CERD Committee clarify that government action as well as inaction can violate obligations under the convention – there is no excuse for complacency or indifference by a government toward either public or private discrimination, particularly when this involves violence.

The 55 members of the OSCE have repeatedly committed themselves to combating antisemitism. In the concluding document of the Copenhagen Human Dimension Conference in 1990, the OSCE members:

> clearly and unequivocally condemn totalitarianism, racial and ethnic hatred, anti-Semitism, xenophobia and discrimination against anyone as well as persecution on religious and ideological grounds. [paragraph 40]

and commit themselves to:

> "take appropriate and proportionate measures to protect persons or groups who may be subject to threats or acts of discrimination, hostility or violence as a result or their racial, ethnic, cultural, linguistic or religious identity, and to protect their property." [paragraph 40 (2)]

The OSCE Ministerial Council at the 2002 Porto meeting issued Decision No. 6 on Tolerance and Non-Discrimination calling on member states "to investigate promptly and impartially acts of violence, especially where there are reasonable grounds to suspect that they were motivated by aggressive nationalism, racism, chauvinism, xenophobia, anti-Semitism and violent extremism, as well as attacks motivated by hatred against a particular religion or belief, and to prosecute those responsible in accordance with domestic law and consistent with relevant international standards of human rights" (paragraph 9).[112] The OSCE Ministerial Council at the 2003 Maastricht meeting issued Decision No. 4 on the same issue, "encourag[ing] all participating States to collect and keep records on reliable information and statistics on hate crimes, including on forms of violent manifestations of racism, xenophobia, discrimination, and anti-Semitism..." (paragraph 6).[113]

# A "New Antisemitism"?

The rise in antisemitic violence in European countries over the past few years has engendered a debate not only about the appropriate response, but about the phenomenon itself. Many observers have described what they call a "new antisemitism," tied to the Middle East conflict and grounded in attacks on Israel.[114] A correlation between surges in violent attacks on Jews in Europe with escalating violence in the Israel-Palestine conflict has been a factor in this debate.[115] Similarly, the role of members of Europe's immigrant Muslim communities in many attacks on Jews, particularly in France, has been cited. Antisemitic propaganda flowing from the Middle East also is mentioned as further evidence that Europe is facing a "new antisemitism."

The argument that antisemitism is in some way an inevitable side-effect of the Middle East conflict and opposition to actions by the government of Israel has, in some cases, been seized upon by European governments to justify not outrage but inaction. The involvement of European Muslims and immigrants in many incidents, in turn, has been highlighted by some monitors of antisemitism who tend to identify both the problem and the needed remedy in terms of European attitudes and policies toward the Middle East conflict.

These approaches are unhelpful. Disputes over the proportion of the perpetrators drawn from minority populations, as opposed to "white" European perpetrators, have resulted in harsh criticism of some European monitoring reports (see below). Indeed these have included the insinuation that antisemitism may be a factor in the refusal by some monitoring groups to draw broad generalizations about what ethnic or religious group is carrying out this "new antisemitism." An example cited below is the response to the EUMC's decision not to publish a report on antisemitism it had commissioned.

Reports which have emphasized that the perpetrators of antisemitic acts are of predominantly Arab or Muslim origin have received considerable attention in the news. But in such cases, antisemitism is often wrongly portrayed as a conflict between minorities, and so a lesser responsibility of European government and society. Thus Europe's Jewish and Muslim minorities are played off against each other, even when leaders of both communities make serious efforts to bring them together. This framework actually has emboldened extremist political movements in Europe that are virulently antisemitic, anti-Muslim, and anti-immigrant. Europe's ultra-conservative movements, including neo-Nazi groups, have been encouraged in their cause of promoting racial discord and exclusion. The continued threats of international terrorism, and the horror of the March 2004 railway bombings in Madrid, will undoubtedly further hearten these extremist groups, fueling their hatred of Muslims, immigrants, and other non-European groups, including Jewish minorities in Europe. It will also further polarize relations between beleaguered minorities in Europe.

The torrent of anti-Jewish and anti-Israel hate speech coming through the Internet from Middle East websites is a disturbing and increasingly important aspect of the problem of antisemitism in Europe. So too are the websites sponsored by extreme nationalist and transnational organizations of the extreme right. These latter send messages of hatred that are antisemitic, anti-Muslim, and anti-immigrant. Dutch organizations tracking Internet hate speech have pointed out that some of the most virulent of these sites are hosted in the United States.[116]

There is little doubt that one important factor contributing to the rise of antisemitism in Europe has been the increased violence in the Middle East conflict, and greater hostility toward Israeli policy. But violence needs to be viewed as a part of the larger tapestry of racism and antisemitism in Europe, with all of its history. Governments are more likely to tolerate racist and sectarian attacks against minorities when they are framed as protests against real or imagined wrongs or inter-minority conflicts – whether the targets are illegal immigrants, Roma, Muslims, or Jews.

To some, criticism of Israel is itself a part of the "new antisemitism." Whether – or rather, when – such criticism should be considered a manifestation of antisemitism is hotly disputed. In this debate, criticism of Israel's policies or practices, or of the Jewish national movement, Zionism, is sometimes portrayed as inherently antisemitic. But unfortunately the distinction between legitimate criticism of Israel and antisemitism is often blurred.[117]

Author Bernard Lewis anticipated the current debate in his 1987 book on antisemitism:

> It would be palpably unjust, even absurd, to assert that all critics or opponents of Zionism or Israel are moved by anti-Semitism; it would be equally mistaken to deny that anti-Zionism can on occasion provide a cloak of respectability for a prejudice, which, at the present time, and in the free world, is not normally admitted in public by anyone with political ambitions or cultural pretensions.[118]

Others, more recently, have pointed to a propensity to define any criticism of Israel as antisemitic that sets "the threshold of where legitimate criticism tips over into antisemitism impossibly low."[119] But such criticism which disparages or demonizes Jews as individuals or collectively in attacks on Israel or Zionism – or which takes the form of broadside attacks against "Jews" or "the Jewish State" – crosses the line to become antisemitic expression.

In the lexicon of antisemitism, criticism of Israel can be expressed through advocacy of generalized hatred of Jews, while masking racist violence against a people as criticism of Israeli policies. Inversely, criticism of Israel can be colored and impelled by antisemitism. Recent statements by European leaders and by U.N. Secretary-General Kofi Annan have highlighted the need to draw the line at criticism of Israel that lapses into racist antisemitism.

## Establishing Limits

Increasingly, national and international leaders have condemned attacks on Jews and the Jewish community that are voiced as criticism of Israel or Zionism. These leaders have recognized that public protest is frequently a pretext and a rallying cry for unabashed racist attacks.

In July 2002, the OSCE Parliamentary Assembly adopted the Berlin Declaration, which condemned antisemitism and addressed directly the tendency to excuse attacks on Jews by reference to the Middle East conflict, resolving: "That violence against Jews and other manifestations of intolerance will never be justified by international developments or political issues."[120]

In February 2004 U.N. Secretary-General Kofi Annan addressed the issue head on:

> In some cases, anti-Semitism appears to be a by-product of the Israel-Palestine conflict, particularly with the escalation of hostilities in the past several years. Criticism of Israeli policies is one thing. But it is quite another when such critiques take the form of attacks, physical or verbal, on Jewish individuals and the symbols of their heritage and faith. The situation is painful and complex enough as a political matter, without adding religion and race to the debate.

> No one should be allowed to use criticism of Israel's actions as a mask for anti-Semitism. Nor, on the other side, should Israel's supporters use the charge of anti-Semitism to stifle legitimate discussion. The United Nations, for its part, must reject all forms of racism and discrimination. Only in so doing, clearly and consistently, will it be true to its Charter and to the Universal Declaration of Human Rights, and to people of all creeds and colours striving for their dignity.

In February 2004, President of the European Commission Romano Prodi observed further, "that some criticism of Israel is inspired by what amounts to anti-Semitic sentiments and prejudice. This must be recognised for what it is and properly addressed."[121]

Notwithstanding the public commitment of some European leaders to address antisemitism with new vigor, there is still considerable doubt and suspicion that words will be followed by action. Jewish community and antiracism activists contend that European governments and multilateral institutions like the European Commission are reluctant to acknowledge the "new antisemitism." Jewish analysts point to a political climate in Europe dominated by pro-Palestinian sentiment, an anti-Israel bias in the media, and common-place attacks on Israel that cross the line of legitimate criticism of Israeli policies into antisemitism. At the same time, there is concern that governments have in effect downplayed the significance of the spate of antisemitic violence, attributing the phenomenon too readily and for too long to "hooligans" or "disaffected youth" and thus minimizing its importance as a significant human rights issue.

This debate is increasingly acrimonious. On November 22, 2003, the London *Financial Times* reported that the European Monitoring Centre on Racism and Xenophobia (EUMC) had shelved a lengthy report on antisemitism commissioned of the Technical University of Berlin's Center for Antisemitism Research. The report argued that there was a "close link" between the increase in antisemitism and the conflict in the Middle East; it further noted that an increasing number of perpetrators of antisemitic acts are drawn from Muslim communities in Europe.[122]

Eventually opting to release the 112-page report – already widely available on the Internet – the EUMC published a disclaimer defending its initial decision "to continue research on antisemitism with a view to publishing a comprehensive report at a later stage." The disclaimer argues that the data in the report are "neither reliable nor objective" and points to analytical shortcomings in the report, such as an inconsistently applied definition of antisemitism, unsubstantiated statements of causality, and problematic generalizations about antisemitism within Muslim communities.[123] On the issue of "generalization," the note elaborated:

> That report could be seen as suggesting that individual acts of anti-Semitism are indicative of anti-Semitism being endemic among "Arab/North African Muslim immigrants," "the Muslim population," "young Muslims." Using such broad and general categories seems to be based on the assumption that homogeneous communities exist who share certain traits by virtue of their ethnic or religious background. Such generalizations have always been challenged by the fight against racism and anti-Semitism. It is highly questionable to hold certain population groups collectively accountable for the acts of individuals or fringe elements within those groups.[124]

Coming on the heels of a survey commissioned by the European Commission that revealed that 59 percent of Europeans considered Israel the world's greatest threat to peace, the news of the unpublished report lead to charges from Jewish organizations of an anti-Israel and anti-Jewish bias within the Commission.[125] Edgar Bronfman, president of the World Jewish Congress, and Cobi Benatoff, president of the European Jewish Congress, published a letter in the *Financial Times* on January 5, 2004, attacking the commission for what they called "political motivations" behind both the survey and the decision to withhold the EUMC report on antisemitism.[126] Serge Cwajgenbaum, secretary-general of the European Jewish Congress, told the press "This is just outrageous," "There was a decision to hide the truth and we want to know who took it."[127]

At the end of March 2004, the EUMC published its own 344-page report on antisemitism in all fifteen member states, discussed at length below. Among other Jewish leaders, Cobi Benatoff praised the commission for "its huge effort" and, while reserving judgment on the full report, welcomed its publication: "This report is a balance sheet of what's been happening in the lives of European Jews in recent years."[128]

A part of the balance sheet is that antisemitism in Europe is multifaceted and builds upon layer upon layer of historical prejudice and persecution. Right-wing extremist violence against Jews continues to be a significant problem in many European countries, including Belgium, France, Germany, several Scandinavian countries, and accession states to the in Eastern Europe.[129] In its comprehensive report on antisemitism in the current fifteen nations of the , the EUMC provides evidence to this effect, though it argues that the available data is too limited in many countries to draw any well-founded generalizations about the perpetrators of this violence: "In some countries the data collection is reasonably reliable, in some countries the bulk of the evidence is from victims' descriptions which cannot always be confirmed, and in other countries there is no evidence at all."[130] (This statement, however, appears to undervalue the wealth of information from nongovernmental sources.)

The findings were mixed. While in France and Denmark there was an apparent shift in the balance from traditional right-wing violence against Jews toward the involvement of young Muslim males, the analysis of incidents in the Netherlands showed that in 80 percent of the cases in 2002, the perpetrator was "white."[131] By resisting over-generalization concerning the ethnicity or religion of the perpetrators of antisemitic violence the EUMC was prudent. To the contrary, generalizations about antisemitism in Muslim communities runs the risk of both oversimplifying a complex problem and tarring the concern over antisemitism with racist overtones.[132] In fighting racism there is a real need to avoid discriminatory generalizations that demonize whole communities defined by their religion or ethnicity – not least to avoid generating the very kind of discrimination that we define as antisemitism.

Determining the underlying causes of human rights violations is an important step towards identifying appropriate mechanisms of redress and preventive measures. It is in this spirit that Human Rights First is calling on all national governments and multilateral institutions to improve their data collection on antisemitic violence. However, it is equally important, as we insisted in our 2002 report, that authorities take due responsibility in accordance with their obligations under international human rights law to punish antisemitic violence committed within their territories – regardless of the authorship – without recourse to political excuses.

Antisemitism is a form of racism and religious intolerance that can be addressed within the context of regional, national, and international antiracism efforts based on international human rights standards. Indeed, a human rights approach to antisemitism is helpful in three fundamental ways. First, this approach refers to clear, universally accepted international standards. Second, it establishes the responsibility of individual governments to take proactive steps to prevent and sanction criminal acts inspired by racist – anti-Jewish – animus. And third, it places the emphasis on the respect for the dignity and integrity of the victims.

# Recommendations

## To National Governments

### Addressing the Information Deficit

- Acknowledge at the highest level the extraordinary dangers posed by antisemitism in Europe, and the need for governments to report on it.

- Establish clear criteria for registering and reporting crimes motivated by racial animus (sometimes described as bias crimes or hate crimes).

- Publish regular public reports on the incidence of racially motivated crimes, to include disaggregated data distinguishing the particular groups affected.

### Strengthening Enforcement

- Enact legislation that punishes hate crimes and protects vulnerable communities, in conformity with international human rights standards.

- Ensure effective enforcement of hate crimes legislation, to include monitoring of implementation.

- Enact and enforce legislation that establishes racist intent as an aggravating circumstance to be taken into account in criminal prosecutions.

- Ensure that law enforcement agents are properly trained in appropriate recording of, and response to, crimes motivated by antisemitism and other hate crimes.

- Provide adequate resources and directives to law enforcement agencies to investigate and prosecute crimes motivated by antisemitism and other hate crimes.

## Specialized Institutions and Cooperation with Intergovernmental Organizations

- Create and adequately staff and fund a specialized national body to monitor racism and racial discrimination, with an express mandate to address antisemitism and all forms of racism.

- This specialized body should be independent and have the functions envisioned in the European Commission against Racism and Intolerance (ECRI) general policy recommendations No. 2 and No. 7.

- European Union members and accession states should implement the European Council Directive on Racial Equality by adopting national legislation which would create specialized antiracism bodies.

- Cooperate fully with other governments, European, and OSCE institutions to promote greater uniformity in the implementation of high standards of registration, categorization, and reporting on racist crimes;

- Cooperate fully with nongovernmental human rights and antiracism organizations and with community bodies concerned with monitoring and taking action against racist violence and intimidation.

- Cooperate fully with the specialized antiracism mechanisms of regional and international intergovernmental organizations, in particular the European Union, Council of Europe, and United Nations.

## To the Governments Participating in the OSCE Conference on Antisemitism in Berlin

OSCE member states should take the opportunity of the April 27-28, 2004 conference on antisemitism in Berlin to:

- Issue a strong concluding statement that identifies the effort to combat all forms of antisemitism as a high priority in OSCE countries.

- Adopt a plan of action to address antisemitism in every OSCE country. This plan should include improved monitoring and reporting and the strengthening of law enforcement mechanisms to counter antisemitism and other forms of racism and discrimination.

- Establish a high-level position within the OSCE structure, responsible for oversight over monitoring, reporting, and action on antisemitism and other forms of racism. This official would oversee ODIHR and other mechanisms in their work to combat discrimination.

- Within this framework, ensure adequate staff and funding for the new mandate of the Office of Democratic Institutions and Human Rights (ODIHR) to serve as a collection point for data and statistics on racism and discrimination.

- Empower ODIHR to seek information from each OSCE member state, make recommendations, and issue public reports concerning antisemitism and other forms of racism and discrimination.

# Endnotes

1 "Turkey probes synagogue bombing," BBC News, November 17, 2003, available at http://news.bbc.co.uk/2/hi/middle_east/3279063.stm (accessed March 1, 2004).

2 Stephen Roth Institute of Tel Aviv University, "Antisemitism Worldwide 2002/3," available at http://www.tau.ac.il/Anti-Semitism/asw2002-3/CIS.html (accessed March 10, 2003).

3 "Jewish center in southern French city set afire in arson attack," from AFP and Reuters reports, International Herald Tribune, March 24, 2004.

4 European Monitoring Centre on Racism and Xenophobia (EUMC), "Manifestations of Antisemitism in the 2002-2003," p. 45, citing BESC, available at http://eumc.eu.int/eumc/as/PDF04/AS-Main-report-PDF04.pdf (accessed April 20, 2004).

5 "Belgian police thwart attack on synagogue in south of country," Jerusalem Post, June 14, 2003, available at http://209.157.64.200/focus/f-news/928930/posts (accessed April 20, 2004).

6 Anti-Defamation League, "Global Anti-Semitism: Selected Incidents Around the World in 2002," July 25, 2002, available at http://www.adl.org/Anti_semitism/antisemitism_global_incidents.asp#Belgium (accessed August 8, 2002).

7 At least 12 members of extreme right-wing groups were arrested in connection with the plot. German President Johannes Rau attended the ceremony, held as planned. "Home to Germany's second-largest Jewish community, Bavaria's capital begins construction of a synagogue and cultural center that organizers hope will help the city's reestablished Jewish population flourish and grow," Deutsche Welle, November 11, 2003, available at http://www.dw-welle.de (accessed March 25, 2004). See also

William Boston, "On the March Again? A Plot to Bomb the Site of a New Synagogue Raises Fears that German neo-Nazis are Turning to Terror," Time (Europe), September 29, 2003.

8 Jewish Agency for Israel, available at http://www.jafi.org.il/education/antisemitism/nf/nb.html (accessed March 2004).

9 Union of Councils for Jews in the Former Soviet Union (UCSJ), available at http://www.fsumonitor.com/stories/041204Russia.shtml (accessed April 13, 2004).

10 Anti-Defamation League, "Global Anti-Semitism: Selected Incidents Around the World in 2003," available at http://www.adl.org/Anti_semitism/anti-semitism_global_incidents_2003.asp (accessed March 5, 2004).

11 Elaine Sciolino, "Terrorists in Spain Said to Eye Jewish Sites," New York Times, April 14, 2004.

12 Stephen Roth Institute, "Antisemitism Worldwide 2002/3," available at http://www.tau.ac.il/Anti-Semitism/asw2002-3/CIS.html (accessed March 10, 2003).

13 Anti-Defamation League, "Global Anti-Semitism: Selected Incidents Around the World in 2003," available at http://www.adl.org/Anti_semitism/anti-semitism_global_incidents_2003.asp (accessed March 5, 2004).

14 See, for example, the chronologies of antisemitic incidents presented by the Representative Council of Jewish Institutions of France (http://www.crif.org), the Anti-Defamation League (http://www.adl.org), and the Stephen Roth Institute (http://www.tau.ac.il).

15 CRIF recorded 13 violent incidents in schools in France between March 2003 and February 2004. CRIF, "Listes des actes hostiles," available at http://www.crif.org (accessed March 12, 2004).

16 Stephen Roth Institute, "Antisemitism Worldwide 2002/3," available at http://www.tau.ac.il/Anti-Semitism/asw2002-3/CIS.html (accessed March 10, 2003).

17 Ibid.

18 UCSJ, Bigotry Monitor, Volume 3, Number 38, September 26, 2003, available at http://www.fsumonitor.com/stories/071202Russia.shtml (accessed April 12, 2004), citing Moscow's RenTV. It said a 14-year-old

boy, Aleksey Sapozhnikov, received wounds in his leg and was hospitalized.

19 UCSJ, Bigotry Monitor, Vol. 3, no. 35, September 5, 2003, available at http://www.fsumonitor.com/stories/090503Russia.shtml (accessed April 20, 2004).

20 UCSJ, Bigotry Monitor, Vol. 2, no. 27, July 12, 2002, available at http://www.fsumonitor.com/stories/071202Russia.shtml (accessed April 20, 2004); and Stephen Roth Institute, "Annual Report Antisemitism Worldwide 2002/3," available at http://www.tau.ac.il/Anti-Semitism/asw2002-3/CIS.html (accessed March 10, 2004).

21 Community Security Trust (CST), Antisemitic Incidents Report 2003.

22 Greek Helsinki Monitor, "Anti-Semitism in Greece: Selective Timeline 2002-2003," 11 October 2003.

23 Anti-Defamation League, "Global Anti-Semitism: Selected Incidents Around the World in 2003," available at http://www.adl.org/Anti_semitism/anti-semitism_global_incidents_2003.asp (accessed March 5, 2004).

24 Ibid.

25 "Seven Days of Hatred; Anti-Semitic attacks have been making headlines, but strikes against any minorities – Jews, Muslims, Roma, gays – are all too common in Europe," Time, December 8, 2003.

26 UCSJ, Bigotry Monitor, Volume 3, Number 37, September 19, 2003, available at http://www.fsumonitor.com/stories/092203Russia.shtml (accessed April 20, 2004). This source adds that Latvian Jewish leaders linked the attack to a visit to Latvia by the speaker of the Israeli Knesset the following week and to an uncoming referendum on Latvia's European Union membership.

27 Anti-Defamation League, "Global Anti-Semitism: Selected Incidents Around the World in 2003," available at http://www.adl.org/Anti_semitism/anti-semitism_global_incidents_2003.asp (accessed March 5, 2004).

28 "Vandals Defile Jewish Cemetery in St. Petersburg," UCSJ News, February 16, 2004, available at http://www.fsumonitor.com/stories/021604Russia.shtml (accessed March 1, 2004).

29 See OSCE, OSCE Conference on Antisemitism, Consolidated Summary, PC.DEL/883/03, July 18, 2003 available at

---

http://www.osce.org/documents/cio/2003/08/565_en.pdf (accessed March 2004). Articles 40 through 40.7 of the Copenhagen Declaration (the Copenhagen Concluding Document) concern measures to combat racial and ethnic hatred, antisemitism, xenophobia and discrimination. See Conference for Security and Cooperation in Europe (now OSCE), Second Conference on the Human Dimension of the CSCE, Copenhagen, June 5-July 29, 1990, Document of the Copenhagen Meeting, available at http://www.osce.org/docs/english/1990-1999/hd/cope90e.htm (accessed March 2004).

30 OSCE Ministerial Council, Maastricht 2003 Meeting, Decision No. 4/03, available at http://www.osce.org/events/mc/netherlands2003/documents/files/mc_10 70381302_e.pdf (accessed April 19, 2004).

31 Ibid. In a letter of March 22, 2004, ODIHR First Deputy Director wrote Human Rights First concerning the new mandate and requesting support in the collection of information concerning violent manifestations of racism, xenophobia, discrimination and antisemitism and legislation relating to such crimes.

32 Sirpa Rautio, Head of the Human Rights Section, ODIHR, telephone conversation, March 22, 2004.

33 Romano Prodi, "A Union of Minorities," Inaugural speech, European Commission Seminar on Europe - Against anti-Semitism, for a Union of Diversity, February 19, 2004, available at http://europa.eu.int/comm/dgs/policy_advisers/publications/docs/discours _prodi_en.pdf (accessed March 23, 2004).

34 Secretary-General, United Nations, Delivering Inaugural Robert Burns Memorial Lecture, Secretary-General Annan Calls for Brotherhood, Tolerance, Coexistence Among All Peoples, Press Release SG/SM/9112, January 14, 2004, available at http://www.un.org/News/Press/docs/2004/sgsm9112.doc.htm (accessed March 2004).

35 EUMC, "Racism and xenophobia in the Member States: trends, developments and good practice in 2002," Annual report – Part 2, p.89.

36 See for example, Third reports (of 27 June 2003) on Belgium, Norway and Switzerland, and Second reports on Denmark (16 June 2000), Finland (14 December 2001), Greece (10 December 1999), Portugal (20 March 2002), Ireland (22 June 2001), Luxembourg (13 December 2002), and Spain (13 December 2002). All ECRI reports are available at www.coe.int/T/E/human_rights/Ecri/4-Publications/1-Ecri's_Publications/.

37 EUMC, "Manifestations of Antisemitism," p.15.

38 Ibid, p. 15-16.

39 Ibid. "In Greece, Spain, Ireland, Luxembourg, Italy, Portugal and Finland, there is no systematic monitoring of anti-Semitic incidents, and no reliable research and statistics. In these cases what information exists is gleaned from Jewish representative organisations, NGOs and the media."

40 Ibid., p.15

41 Ibid., p.198

[42] Based on information from the European Monitoring Centre Against Racism, "Manifestations of Antisemitism," 2004.

43 Ibid., p.23

44 Ibid., p.26

45 Ibid., p.27

46 Ibid., p.320.

47 ECRI, General policy recommendation No.7 on national legislation to combat racism and racial discrimination, para. 24, available at http://www.coe.int/T/E/human_rights/Ecri/4-Publications/1-Ecri's_Publications/ECRI_Publications.asp#p541_6007 (accessed March 5, 2004).

48 The following countries have functioning specialized bodies of some kind: Belgium, Denmark, Finland, Hungary, Ireland, The Netherlands, Portugal, Romania, Sweden, Switzerland, the United Kingdom, and Luxembourg. Cyprus, Bulgaria, Italy and Spain have adopted legislation to create such bodies, but they do not appear to be functioning. Legislation is pending or existing bodies are under review for mandate expansion in the following countries: Austria, Czech Republic, France, Germany, Greece, Norway, Poland, and Slovakia. Many other countries have human rights ombudsman: Albania, Andorra, Armenia, Azerbaijan, Bosnia and Herzegovina, Croatia, Estonia, Georgia, Iceland, Latvia, Liechtenstein, Lithuania, Malta, Moldova, the Russian Federation, San Marino, Serbia and Montenegro, Slovenia, Macedonia, Turkey, and Ukraine.

[49] Directive 2000/43/EC, known as the Racial Equality Directive, requires a statutory specialized body to address racism and discrimination. It is binding on  members and the accession states that will join the  in May 2004. The deadline for incorporation into national law was July 2003.

50 Council Directive 2000/43/EC of 29 June 2000 implementing the principle of equal treatment between persons irrespective of racial or ethnic origin, Article 13.

51 Transposition of "Lisbon" Directive (State of play 01/01/04), available at http://europa.eu.int/comm/Lisbon_strategy/pdf/transposition_en.pdf (accessed April 2, 2004). Draft legislation is pending in most other countries.

52 See below, and ECRI, Third Report on Belgium, adopted on 27 June 2003 and made public on 27 January 2004, available at http://www.coe.int/T/E/Human_Rights/Ecri/1-ECRI/2-Country-by-country_approach/Belgium/Belgium_CBC_3.asp (accessed April 12, 2004).

53 ECRI Annual Report on ECRI's activities covering the period 1 January 2002 to 31 December 2002, Paragraph 2.

54 European Commission Proposal for a Council Framework Decision on combating racism and xenophobia. COM (2001) 664 Final. 2001/0270 CNS.

55 EUMC, "Manifestations of Antisemtism," pp. 18, 155. A synagogue in Innsbruck was seriously damaged on July 31, 2002. For the FGA website, see www.fga-wien.at.(accessed March 2003).

56 Ibid, citing FGA reports, pp. 159-60.

57 "Molotov Cocktail Hurled at Synagogue in Belgian Capital," BBC Monitoring International Reports, March 20, 2003, citing De Standaard web site, Groot-Bijgaarden, in Dutch March 20, 2003.

58 EUMC, "Manifestations of Antisemtism," based on information by the National Focal Points of the RAXEN Information Network, p. 37.

59 See the website of the Centre for Equal Opportunities and Opposition to Racism (CEOOR), www.diversite.be. CEOOR "was established on Feburary 15, 1993 'as a specialised public body fighting racism and xenophobia, replacing the Royal Commission on Migrant Policy,'" and publishes an annual report on racism, antisemitism, and xenophobia and complaints registered with it. EUMC, "Manifestations of Antisemitism." EOOR, in its function as the National Focal Point within RAXEN, "points to the fact that there exists presently no monitoring system that could provide reliable and valid data on antisemitism"; p. 242.

60 Ibid., p.42. The website of the BESC is at www.antisemitisme.be. Also cited was the Internet magazine Resistances, www.resistances.be/antisem01.html.

61 ECRI, Third Report on Belgium, adopted on 27 June 2003 and made public on 27 January 2004, available at http://www.coe.int/T/E/Human_Rights/Ecri/1-ECRI/2-Country-by-country_approach/Belgium/Belgium_CBC_3.asp (accessed April 12, 2004).

62 Ibid. This is done through the Act of 25 February 2003 "aimed at combating discrimination and modifying the Act of 15 February 1993 which establishes the Centre for Equal Opportunities and Opposition to Racism." "Articles 7-14 of the Act provide that hatred, contempt or hostility based, inter alia, on supposed race, on colour, on descent, on religious convictions, and on national or ethnic origin are aggravating circumstances in respect of a certain number of offences. These offences are : indecent assault and rape; murder, battery and assault; non-assistance to a person in danger; violation of the personal liberty and of the inviolability of private property committed by private individuals; harassment; insulting the honour or the reputation of a person; arson; destruction of movable property."

63 Ibid.

64 Stephen Roth Institute, "Anti-Semitism Worldwide, 2002/3," available at http://www.tau.ac.il/Anti-Semitism/asw2002-3/denmark.htm (accessed April 12, 2004).

65 "France to Help Finance Jewish Security Measures," Reuters, February 3, 2004.

66 "France vows to fight hate crime," BBC News, November 17, 2003, available at http://www.bbc.co.uk/1/hi/world/europe/3275519.stm (accessed March 12, 2004).

67 "Ferry part à la chasse aux «sales feujs» et aux «bougnoules» à l'école," Libération, available at http://www.liberation.fr/page.php?Article=91968 (accessed April 1, 2004).

68 CRIF, Actes Antisémites Répertoriés en France durant l'Année 2002 and Acts Antisémites Répertoriés en France durant l'Année 2003. Fax from Elisabeth Cohen-Tannoudji, March 23, 2004.

69 Commission Nationale Consultative des Droits de l'Homme, Rapport annuel – La lutte contre le racisme (2002), available at http://www.commission-droits-homme.fr/travauxCncdh/2002/cncdh_rapport_28.html (accessed March 10, 2004).

70 "Les trois quarts des actes racists lies a liés à l'antisémitisme," Libération, April 1, 2004, available at

http://www.liberation.fr/page.php?Article=190983&AG (accessed April 6, 2004); and Sylvia Zappi, "Le nombre des agressions racistes et antisémites a diminué en 2003, mais demuere élevé," Le Monde, April 1, 2004, available at http://www.lemonde.fr (accessed April 1, 2004). See also the website of the Commission Nationale Consultative Des Droits de L'Homme, at http://www.commission-droits-homme.fr/.

71 Sylvia Zappi, "Le nombre des agressions racistes et antisémites a diminué en 2003, mais demuere élevé," Le Monde, April 1, 2004, available at http://www.lemonde.fr (accessed April 1, 2004).

72 "Les trois quarts des actes racists lies a liés à l'antisémitisme," Libération, April 1, 2004, available at http://www.liberation.fr/page.php?Article=190983&AG (accessed April 6, 2004).

73 Ibid.

74 "Mardi soir sur Radio-Shalom, le grand rabbin de France, Joseph Sitruk, a même demandé à tous les juifs du pays de remplacer la kippa par la casquette. 'Je ne veux pas que des jeunes gens isolés dans un métro risquent de devenir la cible d'agresseurs qui, généralement, fondent sur eux à plusieurs.'" Eric Fottorino, "La chronique d'Eric Fottorino, Cachez cette kippa...," Le Monde, November 20, 2003, cited in the online bulletin of CRIF, available at http://www.crif.org/index02.php?id=2046&menu=52&type=Commentaires (accessed March 2004). See also Angela Doland, "France's chief rabbi warns Jews that wearing skullcaps could make them targets," Atlanta Journal Constitution, citing Associated Press, November 20, 2003.

75 Bundesamt für Verfassungsschutz (Federal Office for Internal Security) 2001a, as reported in EUMC, "Manifestations of Antisemitism," p. 60.

76 The government's response to this summary statement, in turn, is included in the report: It found that "The statements... 'that issues of racism ... are yet to be adequately **acknowledged**' and the existing legal framework and policy measures have not proven to be sufficient to effectively **deal with** these problems' *are much too sweeping and do not reflect the actual situation in Germany."* ECRI, Second Report on Germany, Adopted on 15 December and made public on 3 July 2001, available at: http://www.coe.int/T/E/Human%5FRights/Ecri/1%2DECRI/2%2DCountry%2Dby%2Dcountry%5Fapproach/Germany/Germany_CBC_2.asp#TopOf Page (accessed March 2004).

77 Ibid.

78 Ibid.

79 Cited in EUMC, "Manifestations of Antisemitism," p, 58.

80 Ibid., p. 67.

81 Stephen Roth Institute, "Germany, 2002/3," available at http://www.tau.ac.il/Anti-Semitism/asw2002-3/germany.htm (accessed March 2004).

82 Ibid.

83 EUMC, "Manifestations of Antisemitism," p. 131, citing il Manifesto, January 15, 2003.

84 Ibid., citing Il Gazzettino di Padova, November 2003.

85 ECRI, Second report on Italy, Adopted on 22 June 2001 and made public on 23 April 2002, available at http://www.coe.int/T/E/Human%5FRights/Ecri/1%2DECRI/2%2DCountry%2Dby%2Dcountry%5Fapproach/Italy/CBC2-Italy.asp#TopOfPage (accessed April 12, 2004).

86 ECRI, Second report on Latvia, adopted on 14 December 2001 and made public on 23 July 2002, available at http://www.coe.int/T/E/human%5Frights/Ecri/1%2DECRI/2%2DCountry%2Dby%2Dcountry%5Fapproach/Latvia/Latvia_CBC_2.asp#TopOfPage (accessed April 14, 2004).

87 U.S. Department of State, Country Reports on Human Rights Practices 2003, available at http://www.state.gov/g/drl/rls/hrrpt/2003/27847.htm (accessed April 15, 2004). See also DOS, International Religious Freedom Report for 2003, available at http://www.state.gov/g/drl/rls/irf/2003/c10268.htm (accessed April 15, 2004).

88 ECRI, Second Report on Latvia. See also, for background on the situation of Latvia's strong Jewish community, Union Councils for Jews of the Former Soviet Unions, "Latvia--Antisemitism, 1995-7: A UCSJ Report, 2001," available at http://www.fsumonitor.com/stories/asem1lat.shtml (accessed April 14, 2004). This sources notes that Latvian nationality policies, which have denied many Russian-speakers citizenship, also affected many Jews.

89 Ibid., section 24, 25.

90 Ibid., section 26.

91 Ibid., section 29.

92 Ibid., section 57.

93 U.S. Department of State, International Religious Freedom Report for 2003, available at http://www.state.gov/g/drl/rls/irf/2003/24417.htm (accessed April 15, 2004): "Citizens' passports indicate the ethnicity of the bearer. For example, Jews are considered an ethnic group and are listed as such rather than as Latvian or Russian.

94 Centrum Informatie en Documentatie Israel (CIDI), "Anti-Semitic Incidents in The Netherlands," English Summary of the Report for the Year 2002 and the period January-May 2003.

95 CERD, Concluding observations of the Committee on the Elimination of Racial Discrimination : Netherlands, March 12, 2004, available at http://www.unhchr.ch/tbs/doc.nsf/(Symbol)/CERD.C.64.CO.7.En?Opendo cument (accessed April 15, 2004).

96 Stephen Roth Institute, "Annual Report Antisemitism Worldwide 2002/3," available at http://www.tau.ac.il/Anti-Semitism/asw2002-3/CIS.html (accessed March 10, 2004).

97 USCJ, Bigotry Monitor, Vol. 3, No. 50, December 31, 2003, available at http://www.fsumonitor.com/stories/123103BM.shtml (accessed March 2004).

98 USCJ, Bigotry Monitor, Vol. 3, No. 26, July 3, 2003, available at http://www.fsumonitor.com/stories/070303Russ2.shtml (accessed April 20, 2004).

99 USCJ, Bigotry Monitor, Vol. 3, No. 48, December 12, 2003, available at http://www.fsumonitor.com/stories/121203Russia.shtml (accessed April 20, 2004).

100 Ibid.

101 Cited in UCSJ, Bigotry Monitor, Vol. 3, No. 30, August 1, 2003, available at http://www.fsumonitor.com/stories/080103Russia.shtml (accessed April 20, 2004).

102 CERD, Concluding observations of the Committee on the Elimination of Racial Discrimination : Russian Federation, March 21, 2003. (CERD/C/62/CO/7 (Concluding Observations/Comments), available at http://www.unhchr.ch/tbs/doc.nsf/(Symbol)/CERD.C.62.CO.7.En?Opendo cument (accessed March 24, 2004).

103 U.S. Department of State, International Religious Freedom Report for 2003, available at http://www.state.gov/g/drl/rls/irf/2003/24430.htm (accessed April 15, 2004).

104 "Human rights groups launch racism monitoring project," Associated Press, September 18, 2003.

105 EUMC, "Manifestations of Antisemitism," p. 187.

106 CST, Antisemitic Incidents Report 2002.

107 Jewish Telegraphic Agency, Richard Allen Greene, "Anti-Semitic incidents up in Britain; Middle East tensions seen as culprit," February 22, 2004.

108 Cited in Sharon Sadeh and agencies, "UK sees sharp rise in anti-Semitic incidents," May 4, 2003, Haaretz.com, available at http://www.haaretz.com/hasen/pages/ShArt.jhtml?itemNo=289724&contr assID=1 (accessed April 6, 2004).

109 Rajeev Syal, "Prominent Jews targeted by Muslims and the far Right," Daily Telegraph, February 15, 2004, available at http://www.telegraph.co.uk/news/main.jhtml?xml=/news/2004/02/15/njew 15.xml (accessed April 5, 2004).

110 Ibid.

111 Anthony Julius, Robert S. Rifkind, Jeffrey Weill, and Felice D. Gaer, "Antisemitism: An Assault on Human Rights," The Jacob Blaustein Institute for the Advancement of Human Rights, August 2001 available at http://www.ajc.org/InTheMedia/PubAntisemitism.asp?did=419 (accessed March 15, 2004).

112 OSCE Ministerial Council, 2002 Porto meeting, Decision No. 6, available at http://www.osce.org/events/mc/portugal2002/documents/files/mc_10395 31872_e.pdf (accessed April 8, 2004).

113 OSCE Ministerial Council, 2003 Masstricht meeting, Decision No. 4, available at http://www.osce.org/events/mc/netherlands2003/documents/files/mc_10 70381302_e.pdf (accessed April 8, 2004).

114 See, for example, Phyllis Chesler, *The New Antisemitism: The Current Crisis and What We Must Do About It*, (New York: Jossey-Bass, 2003); Abraham Foxman, *Never Again? The Threat of the New Anti-Semitism* (San Francisco: Harper, 2003).

115 Peaks of antisemitic violence in parts of Europe, for example, have coincided with the beginning of the Al-Aqsa-Intifada in October 2000, events such as the Israeli raid on the Jenin refugee camp in April 2002, as well as the beginning of the war in Iraq in March 2003.

116 On the extreme right web forum Polinco, see "Complaints Bureau for Discrimination on the Internet, Annual Report 2002," available at http://www.inach.net/content/MDI-annual-report-2002.pdf (accessed March 24, 2004).

117 See, for example, EUMC, "Manifestations of Antisemitism," which includes sections on "The debate on 'new antisemitism,'" and "The debate on antisemitism and anti-Zionism," including a review of the literature (pp. 228-241).

118 Bernard Lewis, *Semites and Anti-Semites* (New York: W.W. Norton and Company, 1987), p. 22-23.

119 Antony Lerman, "Sense on Antisemitism," Prospect Magazine, August 2002 (Issue 77).

120 Berlin Declaration of the OSCE Parliamentary Assembly and Resolutions Adopted During the Eleventh Annual Session, Adopted July 10, 2002, available at http://www.osce.org/news/generate.php3?news_id=2582 (accessed March 2004).

121 Romano Prodi, "A Union of Minorities."

122 EUMC, "Manifestations of antisemitism in the European Union," First semester 2002, pp.16-17, 21, http://eumc.eu.int/eumc/material/pub/FT/Draft_anti-Semitism_report-web.pdf (accessed March 23, 2004)

123 Ibid., Disclaimer accompanying report, available at http://eumc.eu.int/eumc.FT.htm (accessed March 23, 2004).

124 Ibid.

125 "Israeli anger over 'threat' poll," BBC News, November 3, 2003, available at http://news.bbc.co.uk/2/hi/middle_east/3237377.stm (accessed March 5, 2004).

126 Richard Bernstein, "European Commission Resets Antisemitism Seminar," New York Times, January 8, 2004.

127 Mark Perelmen, " Accused of Burying Report on Antisemitism Pointing to Muslim Role," Forward, November 28, 2003. The same source cites one of the authors of the report, Werner Bergman, who said: "They are fearing that the report will discriminate against Muslim minorities and that this would show that the  was siding with Israel," Bergman said. "They put the blame on us because they can't admit they buried the report for political reasons.

128 Cited in "EUMC Antisemitism reports: 'An excellent piece of work,'" EUMC Media Release, April 2004.

129 The following countries will officially join the on May 1, 2004: Poland, the Czech Republic, Slovakia, Hungary, Slovenia, Latvia, Lithuania, Estonia, Malta, and Cyprus.

130 EUMC, "Manifestations of Antisemitism," p.22.

131 Ibid., p. 292.

132 The country sections of the draft report commissioned but rejected by the EUMC from the Berlin Technical University provide some examples of this. The Netherlands section, for example, repeatedly characterizes perceived perpetrators in reported incidents in starkly racial terms, for example, by asserting that anti-Israel protesters were not "native-born":

During the pro-Palestinian demonstration in Amsterdam on 13 April 2002, 75 swastikas were carried amongst the 15,000-20,000 participants, *almost 90% of whom were not native Dutch*; Israeli and American flags were also burned *200 mostly non-native Dutch Moroccan young people* were responsible for the excesses during the demonstration. [Emphasis added.]